LOVED *to* LIFE

Keys to Supernatural Transformation in Your Life

THOMAS *and* JENNIFER ATWATER

MILWAUKEE, WISCONSIN, U.S.A.

Unless otherwise noted, all scripture versions are taken from THE HOLY BIBLE, NEW INTERNATIONAL VERSION®, NIV® Copyright © 1973, 1978, 1984, 2011 by Biblica, Inc.® Used by permission. All rights reserved worldwide. "New International Version" and "NIV" are registered trademarks of Biblica, Inc.®.

Scripture quotations marked NLT are taken from the Holy Bible, New Living Translation, copyright © 1996, 2004, 2015 by Tyndale House Foundation. Used by permission of Tyndale House Publishers, Inc., Carol Stream, Illinois 60188. All rights reserved. TYNDALE, New Living Translation, NLT, and the New Living Translation logo are registered trademarks of Tyndale House Publishers, Inc.

Scripture quotations marked NKJV are taken from the New King James Version®. Copyright © 1982 by Thomas Nelson. Used by permission. All rights reserved.

All emphasis within scripture quotations are the author's own.

This is a non-fiction work. The author and publisher make no guarantees or warranties to the accuracy of the information contained in this book and some of the names and places have been changed to protect their privacy. This book is based on the experience of certain individuals. Every effort has been made to ensure accuracy.

Web addresses or links provided in this book may no longer be valid since the publication date due to the dynamic nature of the Internet.

Editor: Jennifer Atwater
Front cover photograph image by Abigail Atwater
Cover and layout by Josep Book designs
Author Photo by Babboni Photography https://babbonis.com/

ISBN: 978-0-578-74290-8 (Paperback)
ISBN: 978-1-7355563-0-7 (Hardcover)
ISBN: 978-1-7355563-1-4 (eBook)

Library of Congress Control Number: 2020915202

First printing edition 2020.

Printed by Kindle Direct Publishing, an http://Amazon.com company.
Printed in the United States of America

Publisher Address:
7426 Wellauer Drive
Milwaukee, WI 53213
USA
www.911life.org

Endorsements

Over the years, I've learned that you only have authority over what you love. People usually don't care about how much you know until they first know how much you care. Love is the language blind eyes can see and deaf ears can hear. This book will be a guide to help you receive, become, and release the Father's love to the world around you. Are you ready to receive your upgrade in love?

Leif Hetland
President, Global Mission Awareness
Author, *Seeing Through Heaven's Eyes* and *Called to Reign*
www.globalmissionawareness.com

Now more than ever we need this story and this testimony of *Loved to Life* to inspire the world to move from extravagant love for God to extravagant love for people.

Sean Feucht
Founder, Burn 24-7, Light a Candle, and Hold the Line
Author, *Fires and Fragrance, Integrity, Culture of Revival,* and *Worship the King*
www.seanfeucht.com

Loved to Life is a beautiful tapestry of testimonies and lessons from the mission field interwoven with the Scriptures and sealed by the Holy Spirit. Tom and Jen have written a beautiful account of how we as Christians must live from the Great Commandment to the Great Commission. How can we make disciples of all nations if we are not first seeking to love God with all our being and to love our neighbors?

That the mission field is a great teacher of love is evident both in Tom and Jen's life and in the pages of this book. That being said, *Loved to Life* is not a book solely for missionaries but for all Christians! The Father heart of God, the saving grace of Jesus, and the powerful move of the Spirit is found on every page. We know Tom and Jen personally and I highly recommend this book not only for the richness of the text but also because it represents the fruit of their lives in faithful service of Jesus.

Nic Billman
Founder and Director, Shores of Grace Ministries
Author, *Between the Flowers and the Broken*
www.shoresofgrace.com

Tom and Jen Atwater's debut book *Loved to Life* tells an extremely compelling story of a missionary family who left the comforts of the USA to live among the broken in one of the most dangerous and dark places on the planet - Colombia, South America.

Cuidado (Careful)! *Loved to Life* will elicit an emotional and spiritual response from you. Provocative places filled with unusual characters are met by a tall, white man with a smile on his face. What is he doing there? Simply, uniquely loving each person with a heart to express to them their value. This value was given to them from a caring Heavenly Father who loves them for who they are but wants to show them the beauty of His Kingdom.

This is "Lifestyle Missions" at its finest, where the Gospel is not only preached but is demonstrated by a family compelled by love to heal damaged hearts. From street gangs and hitmen to witches and shamans, no one can escape this ridiculous love. The stories along with skillfully crafted teachings and action items will touch your heart and challenge your comfort. When you are finished you may hear the question, "Will you go?" Hágale pues!

Dr. Roddie Nelson, Ph.D.
Lifestyle Entrepreneur

Founder, "Vertical" leadership platform
Author, *No More Excuses: 31 days for a Lifestyle Transformation*
www.roddienelson.com

As an itinerant minister, I have visited and ministered many times at the center described in this book. I can attest to the fact that it is a shining light in the midst of a poor, gang-ridden, drug-infested part of Medellín. I, and the teams I have brought with me, have seen the incredible work they do there....but more importantly, we have witnessed the incredible love and power of Jesus to literally bring light to people and a community that so needs Him.

I read the stories with tears in my eyes because of the hope and encouragement the different stories raised by telling "the power of the testimony." This is such an easy book to read, displaying the Gospel without being "preachy." The stories draw you in, and then the truth of the Gospel captures you. They gently show how a loving Father sent His son, Jesus, to bring love and healing to this community, not through super stars of religion, but through ordinary people, in relationship with the Lord, loving on people and allowing the power of God to flow through them.

At a time when the world needs hope more than ever, this book will capture your heart, and may challenge you to believe that God wants to flow through even someone like.....YOU!

Bill Dew
Founder, Dewnamis Ministries, Inc.
Author, *Living the Miraculous Life*
www.dewnamis.com

We have been in relationship with Tom and Jen since 2011, first through Viento Fresco and now through 911 Life. We have sponsored their mission ever since we met them, which should say a lot about them and how much we believe in them. We have truly never met a couple that has impacted our mission teams like the Atwaters.

They are an inspiration to us and our ministry. Their dedication to not only organize mission trips, but also train our teams in the heart of ministry abroad and how to love well is paramount. They take love extremely seriously, and this is why the Father seems to continue to pour out blessings on them and their ministry. The streets of Medellín, Colombia, are in such need of God's love, and it is evident that the mission of the Atwaters is making an eternal difference through the children, youth, and parents there.

Our mission teams could write pages of testimonies from what they've learned, seen, and experienced in Colombia over the years through the leadership of Tom and Jen. We are amazed at the impact that it has had on our teams back home after the trips. We would call it "transformational," and we don't use that term lightly. Our teams will never be the same.

Tom and Jen treat short-term mission teams as if they are lifelong missionaries-in-training, which they are, no matter where they end up in the future. *Loved to Life* is not only the title of this fantastic book, but it is truly the way I would caption the Atwater's lives. This is the transformational power that drives them every day as they embark on their mission of love to those that need it the most.

Do yourself a favor and read this book from cover to cover. I know it will impact the way you see the world around you and bring you closer to Jesus personally. You will likely want to recommend it to friends as well!

James and Tracy Boyd
Lead Pastors, Grow Church, Naples, FL
Author (Tracy), *Live Again*
www.growchurch.com

"If you need a best friend, Jen will be your best friend. If you need a father for your children, I'll be that father. If you need a place to live...everything we have is yours." This sums up everything you need to know about Tom and Jen Atwater. This book is the fruit of people whom God has used to "love ridiculously." The miracles in this book are inspiring. The lessons in the love behind those miracles are life shifting. You will reimagine the impact of God's love through you in even the briefest moments.

Doug Crew
President, Shiloh Place Ministries
www.shilohplace.org

Loved to Life is such an appropriate title for this book. Every story reflects who Jesus is, and who Tom and Jen Atwater are. I first met Tom and Jen in 2017, and within minutes was in love with them both. There are only a few people in my life that genuinely and purely love like these two. As you read this book, you will understand in a deeper way the power of love to transform a life, and the imperative plea to bring the Father's love to Colombia and the world.

Ron Book
Co-director, Bethel Atlanta Missions

Loved to Life is written with excellence. What a joy to read the testimonies and realize even more how the hand of God is upon Tom and Jen to do the "even greater works." I am thankful they included their own story of following the trail of His glory dust and validated with Scripture the infilling of the Holy Spirit in their own lives. Miracles, signs, and wonders accompany telling the good news of the Gospel of Christ. Tom and Jen Atwater are rooted and grounded in His love and have only begun to experience all that God has for them, which will keep them in awe and wonder of our great God.

Carolyn Book
Co-director, Bethel Atlanta Missions

I strongly recommend you read the book of my dear friends Thomas and Jennifer Atwater. They are laid down lovers of Jesus, and this love of Christ immersed in them reflects outwardly for all to behold. Having known these missionaries to Medellín, Colombia, for some time now, I can attest that their life embodies the message of LOVE at such a critical time.

According to the Hebraic concept, "knowledge" means intimacy, both experiential and practical. Knowledge is not just information, but a message, an ideology that you become. Tom and Jen's message in *Loved to Life* is the culmination of who they are. I believe it's not a book you'll just read and set aside, but that the message it carries will transform you to greater depths of love. As I read this book, I sat back in my chair and laughed, not because it was funny, but because it was so reinvigorating and revivifying. It literally brought so much love out of my heart! It was energizing because Tom and Jen are so sound and practical.

Over the years, I have read many books about love, but I have never read one like this. I believe when you read it, you will embrace it and become the message it carries. This book is both spiritual and practical. It is hands-on and will help break the ignorance and arrogance that foster hate. It's a timely book for today's world. You'll want to share *Loved to Life* with your friends and family and anyone that desires to see what love looks like.

David Sylvester
Missions Director, TOJCM, Scarborough, ON Canada

I first met Tom and Jen during a short-term mission trip to Colombia while leading a ministry team from Gateway Church. In just a few short days, their lives and example had such an incredible impact on myself and our team. Tom and Jen live this message of *Loved to Life* in their ministry, family, and relationships with others. Their heart to love and serve the people and children of Colombia is inspiring and contagious! In *Loved to Life*, they blend real life stories and testimonies with powerful and life-changing Biblical truths. The Action Challenges at the end of each chapter are so helpful in applying these truths in your own life. I enjoyed taking these challenge questions into my devotional times with the Lord. I am so grateful for Tom and Jen capturing in book form what God has taught them in their journey.

Jeremy Meister
Pastor, Gateway Church, Dallas, TX

The very essence of God is love. We hear it taught in precept. Tied closely to Scripture, Tom and Jen Atwater flesh it out for us through gripping, real-life "street" stories in *Loved to Life*. The Action Challenges after each chapter make it practical. Brace yourself for the miraculous when God's love is unleashed! The Father's heart to heal us and others is the clarion call of this book. I've experienced healing from both soulish wounds and bodily ailment through the Atwater's ministry in Medellín. Their message will put wind under your wings, as it did for me, through God's baptism of love.

Mark Cathey
International Supervisory & Care Team, Novo

Loved to Life will inspire you to action through seeing people the way Jesus does. Tom and Jen Atwater are two that are moved by the compassion of the heart as well as the conviction of the Spirit.

William Wood
Global Associate, Global Awakening
Author, *Walking in the Wilderness*
www.globalawakening.com/williamwood

The first time I met Tom and Jen I couldn't help but notice the love of Jesus that flowed through their pores. They were so contagious, evident, and genuine, and I have seen few people with this same passion.

Before reading this book my expectations were very high because I knew that it would provide a scent from Heaven that would infect thousands of people. *Loved to Life* will lead you into a real experience about love so that you will deeply understand the ministry of Jesus.

Sometimes we think the main essence of Jesus' ministry is miracles and power, but in reality, power without love is like a good dinner without substance. It can look very delicious but doesn't taste like anything. In this book you will find a door to the Supernatural with incredible substance.

You will see the same love of Jesus that made miracles, signs, and wonders occur, and you will see the greatest expression of love - the cross. God is going to take you on an incredible journey through this book and I assure you that it will mark your heart in such a profound way that you will never be the same.

Daniel Cortes
Lead Pastor, Iglesia Espíritu Fresco
www.familiaespiritufresco.com

Since I first heard their story, I have been blessed and inspired by Tom and Jen Atwater. There are few people I know who have given more to see broken hearts healed. In reading through their stories and the revelations within them, I hope that you discover how easy it can be to release the transformational power of God's love wherever you are.

Blake Healy
Director, Bethel Atlanta School of Supernatural Ministry
Author, *The Veil, Profound Good* and *Indestructible*
www.bethelatlanta.com/blake-healy/

Contents

Preface

On a balmy Colombian summer night in 1995, we were walking along the cobblestone streets of the old city of Cartagena, Colombia, where I (Tom) had accepted a job teaching English as a Second Language. Suddenly, up ahead we saw what appeared to be a brown paper bag lying on the sidewalk. Approaching it, I lifted my foot, ready to kick it out of our way, when we saw to our disbelief that it was actually a young child sleeping in the bag on the sidewalk!

We stood there for several moments, considering our options. Should we bring him back to our hacienda? Would that be even worse for him, knowing a soft bed for one night and then having to return to the streets? Would that possibly endanger us? Not knowing what else to do, we emptied our pockets and slipped the money underneath him. After a few moments, we walked away from that young child with our hearts forever changed, awakened to the reality of the miserable lives of street children.

A few months later we returned to the United States and continued on with our lives. However, the image of that child on the streets never left us, and the seed that had been planted gradually grew roots which took a firm hold in our hearts.

Over the course of almost fifteen years, God moved in incredible ways that rocked our world and strengthened our faith. He brought us to the place in our lives where we were ready to let go of everything that was familiar and comfortable and move to Colombia to live and serve Him.

We have been living in Medellín, Colombia, since 2011, serving hundreds of the city's most vulnerable children and families, first as directors of a local children's foundation called Viento Fresco (2011-2018), and now as directors of 911 Life Ministries, which we founded in August 2018.

Acknowledgements

Although this book came out of my (Tom's) heart, I could not have written it without the partnership and help of Jen as co-author, editor, friend, and wife. It has only been through the grace of God and Jen's constant, unfailing encouragement that this book has been birthed. If there were ever a Proverbs 31 wife, it's Jen. In the beginning I wanted her to write this book because she's a much better writer. However, she insisted that these words must also come from me and my heart. She believed in me when I did not even believe in myself. She is a gifted writer with prophetic and logical insight and is also the most positive and pleasant person I have ever known.

Bill Dew's prophetic word, "God says to write the book," convinced me that the idea was from God. It kept me going and was the divine encouragement I needed in order to pursue blessing others through sharing these stories.

We want to thank Andrew and Kathy McMillan, apostles, pastors, and founders of the church Comunidad Cristiana de Fe and of Viento Fresco (Fresh Wind) Children's Foundation. Their love, leadership, encouragement, and friendship has blessed us in so many ways, and many of the testimonies in this book were possible because of the doors they opened for us in Colombia.

Special thanks go to Francy Burbano who has been a faithful friend, coworker, and prophetic intercessor throughout our time in Colombia. As the Teacher Coordinator at the children's center where many of these testimonies occurred, she was involved in several of the miraculous stories documented in this book. We worked together in one of the most difficult environments imaginable - a spiritual war zone. Her prophetic insight and diligent labor moved Heaven and helped transform even the hardest cases. Francy, you are a rare and wonderful treasure of God!

Throughout the years, Elmbrook Church and Helping Hands Missions have been faithful partners of our family and ministry, supporting and loving us throughout our time in Colombia. It's because of their partnership that we were able to build houses for the gang leaders and impoverished people you will read about in these pages. They have also provided valuable spiritual and emotional encouragement throughout the years, and their sowing in Colombia has produced incredible fruit!

We want to thank each of the many churches that have sown in us and/or sent short-term teams to visit us. Your partnership brings great spiritual encouragement and leaves an extraordinary impact on our family, ministry, and the community around us.

Thank you to Maria Terreros for her amazing Spanish translation work, and to Jeins Duran for his incredible editing skills, which helped improve both the Spanish and English versions. Your talent and creativity helped make this book shine.

These acknowledgements would not be complete without including our marvelous Colombian team! You are all amazing people who have served with us in Colombia as employees, volunteers, and/or friends. You know who you are, and the stories in this book are your stories too! You are and have been an integral part of our lives, and without your hard work, prayers, and friendship, this book would not have been possible.

Most importantly, we thank Papa God for radically loving us to life, and then helping us to do the same to others. You are everything!

Introduction

This book was written with two purposes in mind. First and most importantly, it is intended to bring you into a closer relationship with the King of kings. Our desire is that you will be transformed and "loved to life" through the stories of hope and miraculous intervention found in these pages. We pray that you will receive a divine impartation and revelation of God's love that will revive your faith, give you hope, and solidify your identity as His child.

The second purpose of this book is to inspire you to action. We want you to be ignited to love others through acts of compassion like Jesus did while walking on this Earth, and out of that love and compassion will come...*life*. Our desire is for you to get out of your comfort zone, loving others to life just as you have been loved to life by the Heavenly Father! And what is this life? It's Jesus! "I am the way and the truth and the life. No one comes to the Father except through me" (*NIV*, John 14:6).

Loved to Life embodies the two greatest commandments: to love the Lord your God with all your heart, soul, mind and strength, and to love your neighbor as yourself (*NIV*, Matthew 22:37-39). We hope these pages communicate to you that God's love is the motivation, the means, and the goal of every sign and wonder He performs. We experience this love through our daily communication and divine encounters with Him.

The Lord has given us countless amazing testimonies, all of which glorify Him and are meant to multiply in the lives of our readers. This book was written to honor the testimonies He has given us. We want to leave a lasting legacy for our physical and spiritual children which they can teach to their children, and so on down the line. A life sold out to Jesus is worth it, and if God can do these amazing miracles through *us*, He will even do more through *you*!

The title *Loved to Life* came to Jen one day after hearing someone say, "Oh, I just love that person to death." She felt there was a better direction towards which to love people - to life! When God intervenes in a person's life and touches them, they are changed forever. They are *brought to life* by His love. They are, in essence, "Loved to Life." This is what God has done to us personally, and what we always attempt to do to others through His love. We hope this book inspires you to do the same! Enjoy!

Chapter One

HUNTING FOR TREASURE

*"Therefore, if anyone is in Christ, the new creation has come:
The old has gone, the new is here" (NIV, 2 Corinthians 5:17)!*

Looking as though he had lived many years in a short amount of time, the man approached our doorway as two hundred children under five years old were being dropped off at the children's center we were directing in Medellín, Colombia, South America. Every weekday morning this neighborhood street in Medellín was filled with the happy chatter so characteristic of Colombians, but I had never before seen this man.

Peering through the continual ebb and flow of parents and children, I noticed the man was dressed in a soft floral blouse, tight women's jeans, and delicate white sandals. His long hair tumbled midway down his back and he walked with a swing in his hips. The man stopped on the sidewalk in front of our building, watching the children with interest as they entered.

NORMAN

I walked over as if approaching somebody I knew, introduced myself, and asked his name. "Oh, they call me 'Maria of the Neighborhood,'" he answered without hesitation, still keeping his eye on the children.

"Well...what did your parents name you when you were born?" I pressed.

"They named me Norman," he replied.

"Is it okay if I just call you Norman?" I asked, willing to use whatever name he would choose. He assured me that it would be fine. "So," I continued, "do you have children here you're dropping off?"

"No," he replied, not seeing the importance of my question. I waited, but he offered no more information.

"Well...can I help you with something?" I continued, pursuing some explanation for his presence at the door.

"Nope," he responded, peering in through the doorway.

"OK, then...um...what are you doing here?" I asked directly, now requiring some sort of answer.

"Well, I'm not sure," Norman responded, leaning his head to one side as he thought. "There is such a positive energy here that I just like to be around this place. I feel peace here and I don't want to leave."

"Wow, that's great!" I replied with enthusiasm. After all, we had been striving for years to create a tangible positive atmosphere in the neighborhood, which was known for prostitution, witchcraft, drugs, and violence. Tired of hearing about the enemy's plans for the neighborhood, I had gone to the Lord, asking for *His* plans for this place. He'd replied that His plans were for peace, purity, and the power of the Holy Spirit. Now Norman was at my door, telling me he didn't want to leave because he felt such peace!

THE OTHER SIDE OF THE DOOR

A thought popped into my head. "Hey...if you'd like to spend more time here, why don't you come to our Ladies' Bible Study on Friday mornings?" I asked. "It's even *more* peaceful when you get *inside*!" Norman twirled to face me, now giving me his full attention. With vivid eyes and a giggle of excitement he agreed at once.

From the beginning, Norman was an active member of the group. He arrived on time every Friday morning, paid attention, and asked thoughtful questions throughout the meetings. We never confronted Norman about the way he dressed or his feminine mannerisms. Instead, we showered him with genuine love, giving him food when he was hungry and loving him just as he was. What mattered most to us was that Norman saw himself as God sees him: valuable, unique, beautifully and wonderfully made, and created for a special purpose.

Every time I saw Norman, I would search for something to compliment. Seeing him in the hallway one morning in a soft pink dress, I gushed, "Wow, Norman, that's a nice dress you have on! It's totally your color!"

Receiving the compliment with a wave of his hand, he replied, "Oh, this old thing? It's all I could find in my closet today to match my shoes." On a different day, I complimented a delicate pair of rhinestone-studded sandals he was wearing.

I've met few people like Norman. He was cheerful, childlike, and encouraging. Although he'd suffered years of drug and alcohol addiction, prostitution, poverty, and abuse, Norman never failed to treat others with kindness and respect.

One day as I glanced out the door of the children's center, I saw Norman sitting across the street on the curb wearing a fitted yellow tank top, one leg delicately draped across the other. Calling to a woman up the street, he yelled, "Hey baby, you're looking beautiful today!"

It's imperative to understand that in the culture of this neighborhood, a comment such as this is not considered offensive or an advance. On the contrary, it's taken as a compliment. Given the struggles that most of the residents experience, it's very likely that just as a dry sponge thirsts for water, she was longing for encouragement that day.

When Norman called up the street, he was telling the woman, "Girl, you are important! You're not invisible. I notice you, and you're doing great!" My heart skipped a beat and I whispered in my spirit, *God, I want a tender heart like Norman's.* It's so easy for Christians to stay inside the four walls of the church judging the sins of people like Norman, while he's outside doing *our* job of encouraging *others.*

NORMAN'S DECISION

One Friday morning, Norman arrived late to the Bible study. Stumbling through the door, out of breath and oblivious to having interrupted the meeting, Norman grabbed the leader's arm and blurted out, "Do you know why I'm late? While I was trying to leave my slum housing this morning, I couldn't get out because I was surrounded by black demons who wouldn't let me pass. I was paralyzed with fear and didn't know what to do, but a moment later I saw a shining white hand coming through the front door to rescue me. This hand reached out, grabbed me by my shirt, and dragged me out of my house! It led me down the street and right here to this place!"

With tears in his eyes he continued, "When you people open the Bible and start reading, I feel something so wonderful, so amazing, so tangible. I don't know what it is, but I want it with all my heart! *Please... tell me what it is!*" Norman was desperate, the tears now streaming down his face.

The leader responded in a gentle voice, "Norman, it's Jesus. That's Who you feel. Do you want to invite Him into your heart?"

"Yes! Yes! I *do* want to invite Him into my heart!" he cried, like a starving man begging for food. With tears of joy, Norman invited Jesus into his heart. He then looked down with disgust at the feminine clothing he was wearing. "Oh, these clothes make me feel so shameful and dirty!" he cried out. "I don't want to wear them anymore. Do you have any men's clothes for me?"

We rushed to give him a package of donated men's clothing, which he accepted with gratitude. Then Norman addressed the class, declaring as would a soldier who is staking his flag into a conquered territory, "From this day on I will no longer be called 'Maria of the Neighborhood'! My name is Norman, and Norman I will be!"

Many significant changes took place that day. The outside changes were visible to all. Norman's women's clothes were replaced with men's clothes, his hair was cut in a masculine style, and he renounced his feminine mannerisms. What happened on the inside was far more important, however. Norman received a new identity as a son of God, a worthy heir. He accepted the righteousness of Jesus which covered his sins.

The Apostle Paul encourages us with these words: "You were taught, with regard to your former way of life, to put off your old self, which is being corrupted by its deceitful desires; to be made new in the attitude of your minds; and to put on the new self, created to be like God in true righteousness and holiness" (*NIV*, Ephesians 4:22-24). Having repented and received Jesus' forgiveness and restoration, Norman became a new man!

BEYOND THE VISIBLE

When I ran into Norman a few months later on the street, I was delighted to find that he was still dressed and behaving in a masculine way. Not having seen him in a while, I asked if he'd been going to church, and he hadn't. I persisted, "Norman, do you know why it's so important for you to go to church? It's because *they* need *you*, Norman! You have a noble and childlike heart. It's a gift from God, and the people in church need to learn from *you*!"

My experiences with Norman reinforced the truth that God's love doesn't look at outward appearances but instead at the heart. God told the prophet Samuel the same thing while choosing a new king for the Israelites. The Lord passed up seven of Jesse's sons, all young and handsome, all seeming to be good "king" material. However, "The Lord does not look at the things people look at. People look at the outward appearance, but the Lord looks at the heart" (*NIV*, 1 Samuel 16:7b). It was only after all seven of Jesse's other sons had been evaluated and passed by that David, the humble shepherd boy and last of Jesse's sons, was brought to Samuel to be anointed as Israel's second king.

Jesus calls out our *real* identity, the identity *He* has placed in each of us. In response, we need to follow His lead and call out the true identity He has placed in those around us. This experience with Norman highlights the importance of seeing people as Jesus does, through eyes of love and compassion. We're to search with confident expectation for the image of God hidden in them. When we find it, we're to call it out so that they can remember, or discover for the first time, who and Whose they really are.

A KNIFE, A FIGHT...A PEACE EVENT?

Sometime after Norman's conversion, another event occurred which seemed to be heading toward a very horrific public murder. Some sort of response was needed to combat the violence and witchcraft we were seeing and experiencing throughout the neighborhood. In prayer one morning, our team sensed God's direction to invite the Prince of Peace into this tough neighborhood. We decided to host a "Peace Day" celebration which would include all two hundred children in the center as well as their parents or caregivers.

The celebration began with a jubilant and noisy parade through the streets. The children cheered, sang, and banged drums, bringing joy and love to their neighbors, while the staff walked alongside the children and interceded for the neighborhood in prayer. Moments after the parade had finished, we were all outside preparing for the next activity when I heard an angry female voice begin to shout.

NOT WHO YOU ARE

Glancing up the street, I observed a young mother with a toddler in her arms being attacked by a much larger woman. The heavyset woman knocked the young mother and her child to the ground and began to pummel her with hard fists. The obvious irony of this situation was not lost on me. Here we were, hosting a "Peace Day" event to combat violence in the neighborhood, while within a mere block of our event a violent fight was breaking out!

Within seconds, a muscular, angry man ran over to the two women. It became clear that he was the partner of the young woman who was now lying on the ground, grasping her child in a tight embrace and unable to defend herself. The man grabbed the larger woman with both hands, yanking her off the younger woman and child. I was just about to heave a sigh of relief when to my astonishment and horror *he* began punching *her* until she fell to the ground! Once she was down, he continued kicking and beating her without mercy as the young mother rushed her child to safety.

I knew *somebody* had to do something, and *fast*! Because of our event, the street was full of parents, children, teachers, staff, and curious neighbors. I had no way of knowing if those fighting were involved with gangs, drug trafficking, or the mafia, all of whom were powerful people who often didn't have a high regard for the value of life.

BETWEEN THE KNIFE AND THE PAVEMENT

In a split-second I analyzed what would happen if I, the "foreigner," got involved. It's hard to hide when you're the only white guy and also a foot taller than anybody else on the street. They would all know who had intervened and could take revenge on my family and me for getting involved with their dispute. This could result not only in my death but also the deaths of my wife and children.

In the few seconds it took for all of this to cross my mind, I noticed that nobody - not even the Colombian men standing near me on the street - had stepped in to stop the fight. The next thing I knew, I had dashed up the street and inserted myself, half-crouched and half-lying on the ground, between the angry, kicking man and the heavyset woman beneath him.

I held the man off with one arm, pleading for him to stop as I searched his hate-filled eyes for some explanation for this attack. After about ten seconds, to my relief he stopped kicking and punching the woman, although he was still very upset. As he stepped back, I scrambled to my feet, breathing an inward sigh of relief. My momentary relief was unfounded, however, when he pulled a hidden knife from his pocket and lunged toward the woman again in unbridled anger, shouting, *"I'm going to kill you!"*

In an instant, I found my open hands on his chest, trying to prevent him from getting closer to her. As I did this, a few things became crystal clear. First, I had just disarmed myself. My arms were straight out with my hands pressed against his chest, leaving the rest of my body open and vulnerable to his hands and his knife. Second, I could feel his large and rippling pectoral muscles under my fingers, and it dawned on me that this guy wouldn't need a knife to do me in. He could just as easily do it with his bare hands!

UNEXPECTED WORDS

The absurdity of the situation would have been almost amusing if it hadn't been for the knife. I wanted to tell this guy to stop being an idiot and that he was insane for trying to beat up or maybe even kill a woman on the ground who couldn't even defend herself. It was then that a quick and urgent prayer burst from my heart.

I would love to tell you it was a calm and spiritual conversation with my Heavenly Father, but it wasn't. It was one of those one-word prayers, if you can even call it a prayer, and that one word was, *HELP!* This silent prayer went unnoticed by anyone except the One to Whom it was directed, and Who heard it and answered. God performed a miracle and changed the words that came out of my mouth!

I looked the man straight in the eyes and declared from my heart, "You're a strong and valiant man! You're honorable and respectful. This woman may have disrespected and dishonored you, but please don't do this. *This is not who you are!*"

Somehow, searching into his eyes past all of the rage and anger, I *did* see these qualities. As the words left my mouth, my spirit confirmed that they were true. These noble qualities were hidden deep inside this man, underneath his rough exterior, beyond what we see with our natural eyes.

RETALIATION

Moments later, to my surprise and relief he calmed down a bit, stopped lunging toward the woman, and backed away. However, as he put the knife into his pocket the woman on the ground took advantage of his retreat. Jumping to her feet, she lunged at him with rage in her eyes, screaming, "*I'm* going to kill *you!*"

I stared at the woman in disbelief, thinking, *This is unreal! Seriously, woman? You've got to be kidding! I just saved your life, and this man could take us both down with one hand behind his back!* In an instant I wrapped her in a gentle yet firm hug, trying to calm her while my arm covered her eyes, shielding her view of the man.

As I opened my mouth to speak, God performed another miracle, changing my words yet again. "You are such an honorable princess!" I encouraged her. "I know he disrespected you, but you are worthy of honor and respect. *Please don't do this!*"

Looking straight into her eyes, I could see she was not only angry but also frightened. I reassured the woman as if I had known her all my life, coaxing, "Come on, it's okay...it's time to get out of here. Let's go." By this time the man had gone, and the woman eventually calmed down and started toward her home.

That day I'd decided to wear a crisp new white traditional Colombian shirt Jen had given me as a special gift. I looked down to find the shirt torn and bloody. All of this had transpired in a few dizzying moments. Dazed by what had just happened, I thanked Heavenly Father for His protection, and for His grace and mercy in giving me *His* words to say instead of my own.

A KNOCK AT THE DOOR

The following day started out like any other day. There were no crowds of people, no knives, and no violence. I was at my desk filling out some mid-morning paperwork when two staff members rushed into my office. "Remember the guy with the knife yesterday?" they exclaimed. "Well, he's at the door...*and he's looking for you!*"

Here we go again, I thought, wondering what the intention of his visit might be. I prayed for God's help before taking a breath and walking out of my office toward the lobby where the man was waiting. When I saw him, I opened my arms wide, gave him a big smile, and wrapped him in a strong hug. As I did this, he turned to the woman at his side and said, "See? He likes me!" Then he asked, "Do you remember me from yesterday? I was the guy with the knife."

I responded in amusement, "Of course I remember you! How could I forget?"

"Do you remember what you said to me?" he asked. I nodded. "You said that I was strong, honorable, and valiant, and I believed you! Your words caused me to remember who I really am on the inside." He continued to explain how those words had called out his true identity, causing a change in his actions.

Imagine how powerful our words can be when connected with Heaven's call on our lives or on the lives of others. In this situation, God had allowed me to see and call out the hidden qualities in this man. When he heard my words, they resonated within his spirit. The destiny and treasure of his true identity were there, waiting to be called out.

HIDDEN TREASURE

"For I was hungry and you gave me something to eat, I was thirsty and you gave me something to drink, I was a stranger and you invited me in, I needed clothes and you clothed me, I was sick and you looked after me, I was in prison and you came to visit me. Then the righteous will answer him, 'Lord, when did we see you hungry and feed you, or thirsty and give you something to drink? When did we see you a stranger and invite you in, or needing clothes and clothe you? When did we see you sick or in prison and go to visit you?' The King will reply, 'Truly I tell you, whatever you did for one of the least of these brothers and sisters of mine, you did for me'" (*NIV*, Matthew 25:35-40).

In this passage from the book of Matthew, Jesus encourages us to find Him in every person we meet, even if they don't believe exactly as we do. This might seem confusing. After all, we know there are plenty of people in the world who commit unimaginable atrocities. How can a trace of Jesus be found in these people?

We find part of the answer in Genesis, which says, "So God created mankind *in his own image* [emphasis added], in the image of God he created them; male and female he created them" (*NIV*, Genesis 1:27). The image of God is in all people no matter what they've done. You may just need to do a bit of digging to find it.

As we encounter homeless drug addicts in the streets, the first thing we almost always notice is demonic oppression. We'll see the enemy's scare tactics as the demons cause the person to growl, become angry, threaten or insult us, speak in demonic voices and languages, etc.

When we first look into their eyes, it's easy to see all of the darkness and oppression that have surrounded and filled these precious people for so long. However, we cannot allow ourselves to be distracted by these dark tactics. We must look deeper, past all of the offense, the fear, and the attacks leveled against us, choosing instead to believe that the King of kings has put a hidden treasure, a piece of Himself, inside them.

You and I must be confident that the lover of *our* souls is also the lover of *their* souls, no matter how ugly or demonic the manifestation may be. Beauty has been placed inside every person on Earth. It's up to us, the sons and daughters of the King of kings, to draw that beauty out. We must dig until we find it, calling out their true

> *Beauty has been placed inside every person on Earth. It's up to us, the sons and daughters of the King of kings, to draw that beauty out.*

Godly identity and bringing it to the surface. Then, this new Heavenly identity can begin to displace the counterfeit identity the enemy has tried so hard to impose on these beautiful people.

CONCLUSION

You might not have people like Norman knocking at your door or be forced to break up a knife fight, but it *is* likely there are people around you whom you find difficult to love. You might be offended by the way they look or by something they have said to you. I invite you to ask the great Giver of gifts for the spiritual insight and strength to see these people the way He sees them. Look at them through Heaven's perspective and be the one who calls the hidden treasure out!

ACTION CHALLENGE

1. Ask God to bring to mind those who have offended you. Write their names down, and then forgive them by name and for each specific offense, speaking the words out loud.

2. Ask God to show you the hidden treasure inside them. As He shows you their true identity, write it down next to their name. Then be intentional and pray this Heavenly identity into their lives.

3. Quiet your mind and ask God, "Who do You say I am? What is my true identity?" Write down what you think God is telling you. Usually it's the first spontaneous thought that comes to your mind immediately after asking the question. Once you have written the answer down, start declaring those Heavenly truths over yourself every day.

Chapter Two

GIFTS, FRUITS...LOVE

"Do everything in love" (NIV, 1 Corinthians 16:14).

What is the most powerful force in the universe? You guessed it... love! This force is unlike any other. This force, this "love," is a *person*. It is none other than God Himself - the same God of the Bible who gave His only Son for us! The Bible tells us, "God is love" (*NIV*, 1 John 4:8). God's love can be our greatest weapon against the enemy's destructive wiles and our greatest resource for good. We must want *more than anything* to know and share this love with as many people as possible so they too can receive it.

GREATER THAN REVIVAL

Several years ago, Joe Kelly, a great evangelist and close friend, received this word from God: "Joe, despite everything you have done in these last two years, you have failed Me, because you have not loved." This cut into him like a surgical knife. It hurt because he knew it was true.

Joe had attended the Brownsville Revival School of Ministry from 1998 to 2000, during which he traveled to many countries and saw the manifest presence of God at work in the lives of thousands of people. After the revival, he ministered throughout the world for two more years as an evangelist. During this time, Joe experienced every miracle except the raising of the dead.

Blind eyes and deaf ears opened, the lame walked, the sick recovered, and demons fled. As Joe ministered, thousands repented and entered into saving faith in Jesus, and God restored innumerable families. In one meeting, the literal glory cloud of God even settled on the crowd! It's no exaggeration to say my friend moved in a powerful anointing and saw the hand of God work in extraordinary ways.

After receiving those words from God, Joe confessed out loud, "Lord, You're right! I don't know how to love, because no one has ever taught me! My father was an abusive alcoholic who abandoned our family when I was young, leaving me to fend for myself." In tears he continued, "I confess, Lord, that I have become *addicted* to Your anointing. I've paid more attention to the *move* of Your power than I have to You. I guess I feel like I don't have an identity apart from what I can do while under Your anointing. I don't know how to overcome this addiction to Your anointing."

THE HARDEST THING YOU'VE EVER DONE

The Lord responded as a gentle father would, saying, "My son, if you let Me, I will teach you how to love, but it will be the hardest thing you've ever done. You'll have to give up everything you've depended on for your identity. You'll need to trust Me completely." Joe knew his only choice was to agree, and although he was scared, he was also hopeful for the healing God would bring.

God led Joe on a two-year journey into a close and deep friendship together. The Lord took away Joe's dependence and focus on the *power* of God, directing him to focus instead on the *heart* of God and on His great love and friendship. For those two years Joe didn't minister anywhere, nor did he pray for anyone. Instead, he developed his relationship with the Lord through prayer and reading Scripture. Joe came to love and look forward to these daily times with God as one anticipates meeting an old friend for coffee.

At the end of two years, Joe sensed the Lord pressing him to pray for healing for a man who was suffering from fourth-stage terminal cancer. "No, Lord!" he cried. "I don't want to lose my focus on You and become addicted to Your power again!" He continued, "If I have to choose between being used in extraordinary ways by Your power or having this close friendship with You, I choose to be close to You, God." God assured Joe that he was now a different man and wouldn't lose this newfound friendship with God. After resisting and wavering, Joe relented and prayed for the man, who experienced a complete and miraculous healing and is still alive today!

WE'VE DONE EVERYTHING WE CAN FOR HER

One Sunday afternoon not long after that experience, Joe and his family headed over to the boardwalk to spend a few hours by the ocean when he noticed a commotion in front of him. Glancing over with interest, he saw a woman lying motionless on the ground, surrounded by paramedics trying to revive her. A girl who seemed to be the woman's daughter was sobbing with her hands over her tear-stained face. Knowing that the paramedics were attending to them, Joe and his family turned and entered a nearby store.

As they were walking out of the store a few minutes later, Joe noticed even more people standing around the woman, who now appeared to be dead. At this point they were no longer trying to resuscitate her. Sensing a prompting from God, Joe approached the scene and asked the paramedics and the daughter if he could pray for the woman. One unemotional paramedic replied in a matter-of-fact tone, "We've done everything we can for her. She's been unresponsive with no vital signs for about six minutes."

A sudden boldness rose in Joe, and he demanded, "I need somebody to give me permission to pray for this lady *now*!" Another paramedic zipping a defibrillator in a red medical bag replied without making eye contact, "Fine...pray for her if you want, but she's been dead now for a while."

Joe knelt on the wooden planks of the boardwalk, laid his hand on the woman's lifeless body, and began commanding, "In Jesus' name..." Before he could even finish his sentence, the lady jolted straight up and opened her eyes, breathing and alive! Joe was more surprised than anybody by what God had done.

The woman's daughter, still inconsolable, was wailing and rocking back and forth on the boardwalk with her hands covering her face, oblivious to the fact that her mother was now alive. She continued moaning, "My mother is dead! My mother is dead!" Joe took her by the shoulders and peeled her hands from her face so they could see eye-to-eye. He pointed to her mother, saying, "No, look...she's alive!"

WHAT JUST HAPPENED?

As the reality of this hit Joe, he took several steps back, distancing himself from the growing crowd. In amazement, he turned to his family, and asked, "*What just happened*?" They replied, "The *love* of God raised that woman from the dead!" This realization struck Joe like a freight train. In an instant it all made sense, like a lost puzzle piece put in place. It wasn't God's great power, but His *love* for the woman and her family that had brought her back to life!

One might think the driving force behind divine miracles is God's power, but it's not. God's love for us goes first. It is the motivation behind every miracle! The greatest miracle of all is that Father God sent His son Jesus to pay the price for our sins. "For God so *loved* [emphasis added] the world that he gave his one and only Son, that whoever believes in him shall not perish but have eternal life" (*NIV*, John 3:16). His *love* draws us into a closer, deeper relationship with Him, and it was His *love* that resurrected that woman from death to life.

LOVE FOR LOVE'S SAKE

Since God's love always precedes His power, our focus shouldn't be on His power. If love goes first, His power will always follow, but *power without love* does not bring lasting change. Even power that comes from God can be destructive in our hands, while love always brings His Kingdom.

In case you're confused, allow me to explain. When the anointed power of God is in the hands of someone whose heart remains unhealed or who has not been transformed to the core by God's love, this power can hurt that person and those around them. Like Joe, they may feel confusion, seeing their value and identity in terms of how much God's power is manifesting in their ministry. As Joe once told me, "Power for power's sake always destroys, but love for love's sake always brings the Kingdom of God." God's power will always accompany His love, so if love is our focus, we will never fail!

Joe's story exemplifies what 1 Corinthians 13 is trying to convey when it says, "If I speak in the tongues of men or of angels, but do not have love, I am only a resounding gong or a clanging cymbal. If I have the gift of prophecy and can fathom all mysteries and all knowledge, and if I have a faith that can move mountains, but do not have love, I am nothing. If I give all I possess to the poor and give over my body to hardship that I may boast, but do not have love, I gain nothing" (*NIV*, 1 Corinthians 13:1-3).

Let these verses sink in. You could give *all* of your money and even your *life* for the cause of the poor, but if it's not done from a heart motivated by love, your sacrifice is useless! You could heal the sick, move mountains, and have an amazing gift of prophecy, yet if you haven't learned how to love, all of that will gain you nothing. The gifts of God are indispensable in today's world, but if they do not pass through a heart that loves others for love's sake, these gifts end up being more harmful than helpful. *Everything* must hang from love!

CHASING AFTER THE FRUITS AND THE GIFTS

In our ministry, most days we find ourselves in extremely difficult situations. Many times we don't have what it takes to complete the task at hand. We find it impossible to run with the vision God had set before us, or to solve the crises that come at almost every turn. I'm very conscious of my own personal need for Him and for everything He has for me. That's why when I read in the Bible about the fruits and the gifts of the Holy Spirit, I want *every one of them* in great amounts! I run after *all* of them, because I need them *all* every single day!

> *The gifts of God are indispensable in today's world, but if they do not pass through a heart that loves others for love's sake, these gifts end up being more harmful than helpful.*

GREATER THAN THE GIFTS

In 1 Corinthians 12, Paul explains to the Corinthian church about having a balance between the fruits and the gifts. He starts by saying, "Now concerning spiritual gifts, brethren, I do not want you to be uninformed" (*NIV*, 1 Corinthians 12:1). The first step is to know what the spiritual gifts are.

Paul explains that although distinct people often manifest unique gifts, these gifts are designed to work together, because they are from the same Holy Spirit. As brothers and sisters in Christ we need to work together in unity, honoring the diversity of gifts to make advances for the Kingdom together.

After discussing the gifts, Paul points to something even more intriguing when he says, "And yet I show you a more excellent way" (*NKJV*, 1 Corinthians 12:31). What could be more excellent than all of those amazing gifts? What could be greater than healing, prophecy, and miracles? The Bible gives us the answer. It's love! Love is more excellent than all the other gifts in a myriad of ways!

WHAT TO PURSUE

At first, Paul seems to be encouraging the Corinthians to pursue *either* spiritual gifts *or* love, but he later emphasizes both, saying, "Pursue love, *and* [emphasis added] desire spiritual gifts" (*NKJV*, 1 Corinthians 14:1). He is saying that all of the gifts must hang off of love if they are to produce good fruit.

As the following graphic represents, all the fruits and the gifts hang from love, so if you have love, by default you have all the fruits and gifts. It's as if love is the vine, and they are the branches. The branches cannot produce fruit unless they are connected to the vine. This means our primary focus must be love!

LOVE

Distinguishing of spirits · Miracles · Faith · Word of wisdom · Word of knowledge · Prophecy · Speaking in tongues · Interpretation of tongues · Faithfulness · Goodness · Kindness · Patience · Peace, Joy · Self Control · Humility

Our principal goal must *first* be to love the person in front of us - not to heal them, give them a prophetic word, or prove how well we navigate Scripture. We shouldn't first correct them, trying to impress them with our intimate relationship with the Lord or our skillful discourse. Instead, we must empty ourselves of the other motivations of our heart and allow the Heavenly Father to love that person through us. When we do this, we are depending on God and His love, instead of depending on ourselves, to do the amazing and powerful transformative work in their lives.

CONCLUSION

Love is eternal! If you saturate everything you do with love, the results will have an eternal impact for the Kingdom of God. You can preach, prophesy, heal, and cast out demons, but if the person on the receiving end doesn't feel love from you, what are you accomplishing?

When you pray for healing, you must not only pray in faith but also in love, as Jesus did. Compassion is love in action. The Bible says,

"When Jesus landed and saw a large crowd, he had compassion on them and healed their sick" (*NIV*, Matthew 14:14). When Jesus put His love into action, Father God responded to that love through the power of the Holy Spirit. As you put *your love* for others into action, Father God will respond to your love through the power of the Holy Spirit, too! You can't go wrong when your focus is on love!

ACTION CHALLENGE

1. Think of ways you have given more importance to God's gifts and power than to His love and relationship with you. Write them in your journal and ask Him to forgive you. Ask God to take you on a journey like Joe's in which you can develop a deep friendship with God and He can teach you how to love.
2. Talk to Jesus as if He's right there in front of you. Your side of the conversation might sound something like, *Jesus, teach me how to truly love. Show me what it is to love like You do and show me how to love You first.* Listen for His answer and write it in your journal.

Chapter Three

NEVER THE SAME!

*"I have been crucified with Christ and I no longer live,
but Christ lives in me" (NIV, Galatians 2:20a).*

God will often do the most amazing miracles when we are least expecting them. We may be rushing through our day, focused on checking off our "to do" list, when a divine opportunity arises. Often our first reaction is to get frustrated that our schedule is altered or our plans have to change, making us late for our next appointment. I like to call it, "honoring the interruption," because that's what it almost always is - an interruption. However, these interruptions pave the way for God's Hand to move in marvelous and life-changing ways!

EXTREME MAKEOVER

We were in the middle of staff devotions before the children arrived early one morning, and I was sharing about the importance of loving others when there was an interrupting knock at the door. A bit frustrated, I stopped teaching and pulled the door open to find a dirty and disheveled street lady who smelled of filth. Her face was haggard and covered with dirt, and the few crooked teeth in her mouth were stained yellowish-grey. Her torn and soiled clothes were much too large for her frame, and I noticed that there was almost no trace of life left in her blank eyes.

"Can I help you?" I asked in a soft voice.

"Yes," she responded with desperation in her eyes. "I need prayer. Can someone here pray for me?" Her response took me by complete surprise. When people living on the street ask for something, it's almost always either food or money. This woman was different, and she now had my complete attention.

"What is your name?" I asked with a smile.

"Consuelo," she responded.

"Do you have children who attend the center?" I asked. She didn't, which heightened my curiosity. "Why do you think we have prayer here?" I asked.

"Well," she explained in a weary voice, "I'm sick of my life. Everything is going wrong. I'm tired and I don't want to go on living anymore. When I woke up this morning, I decided I would kill myself." Several of our staff members, glued to her words, had stepped forward to comfort her.

She continued, "I was standing on the corner on that busy street where the buses speed by, ready to jump in front of one of them, when for some reason I turned to look up the street and saw a light coming from your closed, windowless door. I thought, 'They are different. They have something I need.' I knew it was God, so that's why I am here. Will you pray for me?"

LIST OF PATHOLOGIES

We brought Consuelo inside and sat her on a chair. A teacher and I had just begun to pray when Consuelo began to list all the problems in her life. They included drug and alcohol addiction, depression, and anxiety. She was experiencing anger, broken relationships with family members, suicidal thoughts, and self-hate. Her physical chronic illness brought pain, inflammation, and stomach and heart issues. The laundry list was much too overwhelming to even begin to address.

Having graduated with a bachelor's degree in Psychology, I recognized a three-feet-long list of pathologies. As a trained deliverance minister, I saw a list of demons just as long. I told Consuelo, "This is above my pay grade, sweetie, but Jesus already knows everything that is wrong. We have to put our faith in Him for the healing and miracles you need."

Consuelo listened as we shared how Jesus had already paid for her sin and disease, taking it upon Himself on the cross over two thousand years ago. We assured her that His forgiveness was free. With only the smallest trace of hope, Consuelo invited Jesus into her heart and together we prayed that He would do the work of restoration in her life.

THE UNEXPECTED

Several weeks later I was crossing an empty street when I saw Consuelo on the other side. As we met in the middle of the street, I saw to my dismay that she looked *worse* than before! The stench on her body and clothes was a combination of garbage, urine, feces, drugs, cigarettes, mud, and filth. Ignoring that, I threw my arms around her in an enormous hug that drew her close. Jesus wanted to express His love and acceptance through me, and she needed to know that her filth would not keep the love of God from her.

Tears streamed down Consuelo's cheeks as she cried in desperation, "Oh, I can't go on anymore! This life is so difficult. It's too hard!"

Compassion flowed from deep inside me as tears fell from my face. "I know, dear Consuelo. I know it's so tough. This is bigger than you or me, but I know One who is greater than all of this, and He is able to take it all away. It's Jesus! Let's put ourselves in agreement that He can do this!"

Sighing with slumped shoulders, she agreed to keep trying with His help, and together we prayed, "Lord Jesus, come! We need You to intervene and take all of these bad things away. Only You can do this!" Consuelo's voice wavered as she prayed, and I could sense how weary and defeated she was.

As I hugged Consuelo one last time and then watched her trudge back up the street, I chose not to let this bring me down. Instead, I placed Consuelo and her problems into Jesus' hands. He would have to take care of her. All I could do now was pray.

UNBELIEVABLE

Several weeks later I was outside the center one afternoon and happened to glance up the street. There I saw a woman strutting toward me with a joyful bounce in her step, smiling as she pushed a cart filled with the coffee, candy, gum, and snacks she was selling. The woman wore a clean pressed blouse and colorful flowing pants, and her hair was washed and combed with care. I couldn't believe my eyes. It was Consuelo!

Joy overwhelmed me as I pointed up the street with an outstretched arm, yelling, "Consuelo, *EXTREME MAKEOVER!*" I ran to meet her, wrapping her in a warm hug. We were both crying as I asked how this incredible change had taken place.

"Look at me!" she exclaimed through grateful tears. "It's a miracle! My addictions are gone. My relationships are all put back together. My heart and stomach have been healed. I've got a job selling coffee and candy. Not only am I no longer depressed, but now *I'm the one who is encouraging all the other people on the street!*"

Consuelo was beaming with joy as she shared this news. I praised Jesus, crying, "Look at everything Jesus has done for you!"

"I know!" she agreed, her face brimming with excitement. "It's amazing!"

CHILDLIKE TRUST

In Matthew 18, the disciples asked Jesus which of them would be the greatest in the Kingdom. He put a child among them and said, "Truly I tell you, unless you change and become like little children, you will never enter the kingdom of heaven. Therefore, whoever takes the lowly position of this child is the greatest in the kingdom of heaven" (*NIV*, Matthew 18:3-4). This is echoed in chapter 19 of the same Gospel, in which Jesus said, "Let the little children come to me, and do not hinder them, for the kingdom of heaven belongs to such as these" (*NIV*, Matthew 19:14).

You must not be afraid to depend on Jesus and trust Him with your future. As you become like a little child, the Kingdom of Heaven will not only belong to you, but it will also manifest in and through you, just like it did for Consuelo!

Another wonderful thing happens as you trust and depend on God: your true identity is called out. Consuelo's life seemed like a mess, but that's not how God saw her. He looked past the dysfunction and the stench on her clothes and found what He had truly created her to be. God saw His treasure in her, her true identity, and He called it out. He moved Heaven, giving Consuelo an "extreme spiritual makeover" and changing her life forever.

Most would say that Consuelo had been beyond help. There may be areas of your life that seem beyond help, too. You may have made bad decisions or experienced atrocities at the hands of others, but *there is hope*! The great Healer, Jesus, wants to heal you and mend the brokenness in your life.

PROPHECY AND A STRIP CLUB

Just as God called out Consuelo's true identity through inner and physical healing, a person's true identity can also be called out using the gift of prophecy. However, this gift can be tricky for Christians who may have been damaged when it was not used in love or humility.

One evening Jen and I were ministering to a small group which included a young man we had just met. Although we did not know it, he was living a life filled with pornography, promiscuity, and alcohol abuse. The Lord impressed the word "purity" on Jen's heart, and she discerned that he struggled in this area. She could have declared him a filthy, dirty sinner, and given him warnings of hell if he didn't repent.

However, Paul points out that "the one who prophesies speaks to people for their strengthening, encouraging and comfort" (*NIV*, 1 Corinthians 14:3). In Colossians we are told, "Above all, clothe yourselves with love, which binds us all together in perfect harmony" (*NLT*, Colossians 3:14). Following this advice, Jen clothed herself first with love, and then whispered into the young man's ear, "I believe God wants to bless you and is calling your heart to greater purity."

FREEDOM

Six months later we saw this young man again, and he confessed that for years pornography and alcohol had been huge strongholds in his life. He'd even visited a strip club the night before we met him the first time, and had been struggling about it with the Lord all that day!

This young man shared that when Jen prayed for him and mentioned the word "purity," he knew with absolute certainty that God loved and forgave him and was calling him to something greater. God cared about the details of his life and was speaking to him in a direct yet loving way. Through this word, he knew God would help him get out of the pit of pornography into which he had fallen and seemed unable to escape.

This young man's life had been transformed from that point forward. As he attempted to avoid the things which had bound him, God demolished the addictions and called out the amazing purposes placed in him while being knit together in his mother's womb. This young man was so impacted by that one simple, kind, and loving word from the Father that he is now being used by God to minister and give clear prophetic words that love others to life. Even more important is the fact that he is now experiencing great friendship and closeness with the loving Father Who saved him!

PROPHETIC IMPACT

When we receive a word from the Lord for someone else, "love" encourages us to give it in wisdom. Prophecy is a means to express the loving heart of God to others. To be effective, it must come from a heart of humility and be enveloped in love.

Two things happen to a person when a prophetic word is shared with them in love. First, the person receiving the word is overwhelmed that God cares about the details of their life. Second, they know beyond any doubt that God loves them. The Apostle Paul tells us, "Do not quench the Spirit. Do not treat prophecies with contempt but test them all; hold on to what is good, reject every kind of evil" (*NIV*, 1 Thessalonians 5:19-22). As we saw in that young man's life, God's love can reach even the most remote and broken hearts, transforming situations that seem hopeless and without remedy.

> *Prophecy is a means to express the loving heart of God to others. To be effective, it must come from a heart of humility and be enveloped in love.*

Some of the most damaged hearts we have seen are those of sex trafficked victims found in cities such as Medellín. An online article published in 2014 by Fox News reported that Medellín, Colombia, had achieved the unenviable title of "the world's biggest brothel."[i] Many of these girls were minors recruited against their will who were unable to return to their families.

Our hearts have always been to help and rescue these vulnerable people, and since we don't have our own rehabilitation center, we partner with other non-profit organizations who do. One is a temporary 24-hour care facility run by the government for minor girls who have been rescued from sex trafficking. The program is intended to be for a maximum of six months, with the girls remaining in the institution until the authorities locate their families so they can be reunited.

THE BACK WALL

One Saturday afternoon we sent a visiting team from the United States to minister the love of Jesus to these precious girls. As thirty of them sat in chairs watching our team perform an evangelistic drama, one team member happened to notice two girls crying far away from each other in the back of the room, each on opposite ends of the last row. One was turned away from the drama and was facing the back wall.

When the team member approached her to ask why she was crying, the girl blurted out through tears, "My life has been horrible ever since I can remember. At a young age I was taken from my family and forced into sex slavery. I lived that abusive life all alone for so many years. Now they've been searching for my family for over six months and haven't found them. I'm past my time here. I have no family to speak of and no friends. There is no one who knows me and can care for me. I'm stranded and alone in the world!"

THE APPEARANCE

The team member prayed for God to intervene in this girl's life. Moments later the girl shot up to a standing position with her arm straight out, pointing in astonishment at the back wall. Bewildered, she shouted, "*Who is that? Who is that?*"

The team member asked, "What are you talking about? I don't see anything."

The girl exclaimed, "How can you not see Him? There is a man with a beard. He's dressed in a brilliant white shining robe. *He just walked out of the back wall* and He's looking at me with the most beautiful and kind eyes!"

The team member replied in amazement, "That must be Jesus! He is showing Himself to you!"

At that very moment, the girl on the other side of the room who had also been crying began to jump up and down, pointing in the same direction. She yelled, "*Who is that man in shining white?*" At this point whatever was happening with the drama had stopped, and everybody's attention was on the commotion in the back of the room.

The team member brought the two girls together near the back wall where they stood staring at the vision of Jesus which only they could see. All other eyes in the room were glued on them. The two girls asked, "That's Jesus? Can we go to Him?"

The team member led them to where Jesus was standing, and the girls fell at His feet and began to weep. Awestruck and in tears, they adored Him right there on the floor as the tangible love of God filled them to overflowing.

Another adolescent girl moved forward and after gaining the courage to speak, said, "I don't see Him, but I want to hug Him. Show me where He is standing so I can put my arms around Him." These girls were so desperate for love and an authentic touch of God that they were willing to hug something they couldn't even see, believing it was Him!

NEVER ALONE

During this encounter with Jesus, a short, sad-looking girl expressed dismay that Jesus must not love her because she couldn't see Him. While talking to our team members, however, she revealed that almost a year before, she'd dreamed about a bearded man in beautiful shining white clothes. Having eyes that made her feel at home, he'd beckoned for her to follow him. The team member assured her that this was Jesus, too!

She asked, "Who is Jesus?" The team member realized that the other girls might not know who Jesus was either, so this was a perfect opening to share with all of them who Jesus is, about His great love for them, and the truths of the Gospel. That day many of the girls repented before the One who had died for their sins so that they might live and receive Jesus as their Lord, Savior, and Friend.

Jesus' message for the girl who felt so alone was that although she may feel abandoned in this world, the God of the universe sees her, recognizes her, and loves her. In other words, she is very much not alone! When Jesus tells His disciples, "surely I am with you always, to the very end of the age" (*NIV*, Matthew 28:20b), this doesn't only apply to them. It also applies to you and me, and to people like this girl at the back of the room who was feeling desperate and alone, thinking nobody in the entire world cared about her.

WHO WILL GO?

Something stood out to me that afternoon. The girl who had received a visitation of Jesus in her dream hadn't recognized that it was Jesus. Since there was no one available to interpret the dream for her, she'd been left in the dark for an entire year. If the visiting team members hadn't left the comfort of their homes for a week to serve others and share about Jesus here in Colombia, that girl still might not know she'd had a visitation from the living God!

If those who *do* know Jesus don't make the effort to share Him with those who *don't*, the world will never know who the bearded man wearing the shining white robe is. Who will interpret their dreams and visions according to the Spirit of God? Who will show them the way to eternal life and a relationship with God if nobody goes?

Will you go? You don't have to become a pastor or travel around the world as a missionary. It can be as easy as sharing Him with your neighbor or the person at the supermarket. Yes, it's risky, and sometimes it's uncomfortable, but the world needs to hear about Jesus. How will they hear if no one tells them?

CONCLUSION

In this chapter we looked at three very different stories of transformation. Consuelo's extreme makeover required me to have an extra dose of compassion and a complete reliance on Jesus. The young man's transformational prophetic word required Jen to speak with love and wisdom rather than criticism and judgement. The extraordinary and breathtaking appearance of Jesus to hopeless girls required the faith and obedience of the visiting team to obey the command to "Go into all the world and preach the gospel to all creation" (*NIV*, Mark 16:15b) so the girls could find out Who had visited them.

> *There is a gold mine of beauty and goodness in every one of us. Jesus sees it even if we don't.*

These are amazing stories of God's grace and loving intervention, and you may doubt that something like this could happen to you. We encourage you not to focus on the results, but on the posture of your heart. In these stories we saw *compassion, wisdom,* and *love in action.* Imagine what would happen if you took faith-filled risks to step out and love others throughout your day!

There is a gold mine of beauty and goodness in every one of us. Jesus sees it even if we don't. As you seek this true God-designed identity in others, you will be able to call it out, handing them over to Jesus to have their lives forever changed.

ACTION CHALLENGE

1. Think of something in your life that has been difficult to overcome. Write it in your journal and ask a faith-filled friend to agree with you in prayer for a miracle. You can say a simple prayer like, *Jesus, this is above my pay grade. I need your help. I need You to move in this area of my life. I choose to believe that You can do this, and I trust that you will. Thank You, Jesus!*

2. It's time to step out of your comfort zone. Ask the Holy Spirit to bring someone to mind who seems to be "beyond help." Write one way in which you can love that person to life this week. Take practical steps to turn your idea into action, following these three simple steps:

   - ACTION: Be intentional in loving others to life throughout your day.
   - COMPASSION: As you step out in faith, be compassionate and do whatever Jesus tells you to do.
   - LOVE AND WISDOM: Allow love and wisdom to guide your words and actions.

3. After you act in faith, journal about your experience, and spend time thanking God.

Chapter Four

PROSTITUTES, ASSASSINS, AND TAXI DRIVERS

*"Go into all the world and preach the gospel
to all creation" (NIV, Mark 16:15).*

Anticipation and uncertainty filled the air as the bus meandered up the hills of the urban mountainside. We were headed to a troubled public high school in an impoverished, crime-ridden, and violent neighborhood. Many of the high school girls worked in prostitution, while the boys either dealt drugs or worked as paid assassins for area thugs. The teenagers were malnourished and suffered physical and verbal abuse in their homes as well. A few years ago, an amazing woman had started a Bible study here, and she was now leading us to minister to these needy youth.

A MOST UNUSUAL SCHOOL DAY

Since neighborhoods such as this are lined with invisible borders controlled by gangs, most of Medellín's citizens avoid venturing in to offer help. We were willing to go but wanted to be sure it was God directing our efforts. When an opportunity arose which we felt was God-directed, we took a chance.

An anointed joint mission team from Colombia and the United States was with us on the bus as we crossed the invisible border into the neighborhood, continuing up the narrow mountain road to the school. We knew they would love these kids unconditionally and minister freedom over their lives. A surprise greeted us as we entered the school. The principal had cancelled all the school's classes for a few hours, making our meeting *mandatory for the entire student body*! Because of this, we would be able to share the love of the Father with five hundred kids for several hours that afternoon!

Desperate to love these mistreated and forgotten treasures of God, our joint team formed two lines facing each other so that as the students entered the auditorium, they would have to walk through our "love tunnel." Our team hooted and hollered, clapped and cheered, and made a tremendous racket as the kids entered! Their faces lit up as we cheered as if they were superstars! These students desperately needed Godly love and attention, and they relished our cheers as they walked, wide-eyed with surprise and smiling from ear to ear, through our "love tunnel."

EVERY HAND WAS RAISED

After the crowd had settled down in the bleachers, a member of our team addressed all the students in a passionate discourse about the love of the Father. He shared how God's Son Jesus had been sent to the cross to pay the debt for all of our sins, and explained that nothing these students had done was too difficult for God to forgive. When the students were offered the opportunity to repent and receive Jesus as their personal Lord and Savior, every hand we could see in the entire auditorium was raised high!

The next few hours were even more amazing. We divided our team in twenty groups, lining them up in the front of the auditorium and inviting the students to come forward if they wanted to receive prayer. Students swarmed to the front, many in tears of repentance, others releasing the pent-up pain of years of neglect, trauma, and abuse. Almost all were crying under the loving presence of God which had descended on the auditorium.

Our joint team loved these students with everything they had, serving as conduits of the loving hand of God. Along with the nearly five hundred salvations we saw that afternoon were remarkable healings, both physical and emotional, and several deliverances. One of the students fell limp under the weight of God's power and was held in the praying arms of a team member for two hours!

The principal paced back and forth on the stage, astonished and touched as his students received the blessing of God. He then asked us to stay later than originally planned so we could pray for all of his teachers, too! Knowing the resistance public high schools generally have to religious activities, we were overwhelmed at the grace of God which broke in to love these dear lost sons and daughters that day.

Later that evening, several parents called the Bible study leader, asking in awe what had happened to their kids. Most of them had arrived home still crying under the presence of God, transformed by His love. Only the God of Heaven can move in such tremendous ways!

GENUINE FRUIT

Seeing so many students' lives transformed by the love of God brought to mind the many taxi drivers I have led to the Lord over the years. Medellín has an abundance of small yellow taxis, and I often take advantage of this inexpensive and convenient way to get around town. Riding in a taxi is a marvelous opportunity to share the love of God with others. The most surprising thing to me is that almost all of them accept Jesus as their Lord and Savior!

There is a culture of politeness in Medellín, possibly due to the prevalence of inexpensive hitmen in the city and the subsequent desire to not upset anyone. At times I had wondered if these taxi drivers were just giving me "lip service," coming to Christ in words alone simply to be polite. One particular day, a taxi driver had just accepted Jesus into his heart. As I rode in his car, analyzing what had just happened and wondering about the genuineness of his conversion, we reached my destination and it was time to pay the fare.

I handed the driver a bill, and when he placed the change back in my hand, I noticed he'd given me too much. I told him so, and his response blew me away. He said with sincerity, "No, you keep it! It's the least I can do after what you have given me! You've given me the greatest and most valuable gift I've ever received: Jesus!"

Let's look at this from an economic point of view. In Colombia, taxi drivers are not very well-paid. Working between twelve and sixteen hours per day, they often don't even meet their daily economic needs. It's safe to say the average taxi driver wouldn't give a customer extra change just to be nice!

This taxi driver's response felt to me as if God were right there in the taxi listening to my thoughts and giving me an instant answer to eliminate any doubt about the genuineness of the driver's conversion. I felt as if God were saying, "Keep it up! Don't stop sharing about Me and bringing in the fish. We make a wonderful team, you and Me. You share My love, and I'll produce the fruit!"

DIVINE DETOX

In another instance when I was riding in a taxi with my wife and kids, I was in the front seat talking to the driver when I felt the urge to ask a very direct question. Confident that God was there with us, I turned to him and asked, "If God were right here in this car between you and me, and you could ask Him for whatever miracle you wanted, what would you ask?"

The car became silent as he thought. After a few seconds his eyes welled up with tears, and he said, "I would ask Him to get me off of the drugs. They're destroying my life! I've tried to quit them, but I can't." Sensing the Lord's hand on this, I told him that God would fight for him, but it would be an easier battle if God could fight from inside the man's heart! I explained that if he asked Jesus in, Jesus could do a miracle in his life.

The driver agreed, and moments after he received Jesus, I put my hands on him and prayed for God to deliver him from addiction. That very instant, sweat began to run down his forehead and face, which was now beet-red, and his entire body began to shake. He cried out in surprise and fear, "What is happening to me?"

I sensed God giving me the word, "detox." I asked the man, "Do you feel peace?"

"Yes!" he replied.

"Do you feel your entire body burning up, but in a way that's not painful?" I pressed.

"Yes!" he replied again, surprised.

I assured him everything was fine, saying, "That's the Holy Spirit entering your life and giving you a detox. Not only is your body going through a physical detox, but your soul is, too! The Holy Spirit will be your Friend and Guide from now on. You must follow Him if you want to stay clean." At this point he pulled the taxi to the side of the road, overcome with emotion, and wept as I shared with him about the reality of God's Kingdom. It's amazing how God "shows up" as we step out in faith and love, praying for those in need!

OUR GREATEST TOOL

The reality and power of God's Kingdom surprised even Jesus' disciples who had walked with Him on the Earth for years. After training His disciples to do the things He was doing, Jesus sent out seventy men to preach the Kingdom of God, giving them authority over the enemy and power to heal the sick. The disciples witnessed numerous miracles as they preached, and upon returning told Jesus how amazed they were at the authority they had over evil spirits. Jesus reminded them, "Nevertheless do not rejoice in this, that the spirits are subject to you, but rather rejoice because your names are written in heaven" (*NKJV*, Luke 10:20).

I believe Jesus used this interaction to refocus His disciples. He wanted them to understand that the true goal and purpose of divine healings, miracles, deliverances, signs, and wonders is to bring *others* into a love relationship with God so *their* names will be written in the Book of Life. He wanted His disciples to understand that the best part about the Kingdom of God isn't moving in the supernatural but spending eternity with Him!

Love is the greatest evangelistic tool we have. We could use fear as a tool, trying to "scare" people into Heaven by focusing on the judgement to come in this life and the hell that awaits them when they die. For some people, however, even knowing that hell is a reality may not be enough to motivate them to pursue a lifetime relationship with Jesus.

As you rely on the Holy Spirit to work in the lives of those around you, your job is to love them to life with a message of truth, trusting that He will do the work of convicting them of their sin. Every person on Earth is already aware of their sin at some level, so we don't always need to point it out to them. As people experience the love and majesty of God, the natural result is for them to feel humbled, convicted, and repentant.

PURE MOTIVES

As Christians we want to see people saved. However, when our deepest motives are to *love them to life*, we can find incredible freedom in evangelizing the lost. We serve as a conduit, helping others have a divine encounter with God in which they *feel* and *experience* His tangible love for them. When this happens, people almost always quit fighting Him, and fall into His loving arms. Then we - the body of Christ - are there to help them understand what is happening and guide them into a deeper relationship with Him.

We see an example of this when people working in prostitution meet the love of the Father. Almost everyone they come into contact with in their day-to-day life wants something from them, whether it be their pimps, their clients, the landlord, or the police. If our goal is to

> *As people experience the love and majesty of God, the natural result is for them to feel humbled, convicted, and repentant.*

get them to say a prayer, go to church, or even go through a rehabilitation program, they are going to see right through our motives from a mile away.

However, if our goal is to approach them in love as Jesus did to the woman caught in adultery in John 8:1-11, we will treat them as real people who have real feelings. In response, they will see our genuineness and be more open to receiving this pure love of God. They may even start to seek after righteousness as well! Ministry to sex workers requires persistence and consistency, along with Heavenly love. It is rarely effective when done through human effort alone.

It's interesting to note that the wealthy often have similar struggles to those in prostitution. Almost everyone with whom they come into contact wants something from them, whether it be their money, influence, power, or advice. Similar to sex workers, they are also adept at recognizing these people from a mile away. Our goal can't be getting them to say a simple prayer or attend church. It must be something much deeper. We have to be generous with our love, not asking for anything in return. This is *unconditional love*, and it's what caused an entire high school to come to Jesus in a day!

CONCLUSION

It would be fantastic if everyone with whom we share Christ enters into a true and lasting relationship with Him, but that must not be our goal. If it were, we would care more about the conversion than the person, and they would pick up on that. Our goal *has* to be to love them and demonstrate God's love for them, right where they are.

Sometimes those we meet will want to talk about their spiritual journey. Other times they won't, yet they'll be happy to hear about *your* journey. Others won't want to hear about either, but if you ask if they have pain in their body or an illness, they will be open for you to pray for God to heal them.

Right now, I invite you to take a chance! Step out in faith and start talking to someone. Ask yourself the question, "What if *this* is the time that God will move in a supernatural way?" Don't waste your time worrying about whether it will "work" or if you might look foolish. Just love the person in front of you the best you can and let God do the rest.

ACTION CHALLENGE

1. The next time you go to the store, break the ice by starting a conversation with somebody you don't know. Then ask, "If God were right here between you and me, what miracle would you ask Him to do in your life?" After they answer, pray out loud in faith, declaring their miracle.
2. Ask God to show you a non-believer who He wants you to reach, whether by sending a text or voice message, baking them cookies, or another similar act of service. Whatever you do, be ready to talk with them about God and their faith if the opportunity arises.
3. Journal about your experiences.

Chapter Five

AT DEATH'S DOORSTEP

"As you go, proclaim this message: 'The kingdom of heaven has come near.' Heal the sick, raise the dead, cleanse those who have leprosy, drive out demons. Freely you have received; freely give" (NIV, Matthew 10:7-8).

A ny miraculous sign or wonder is just that: a sign. What do signs do? Imagine a sign on a highway pointing to a destination. It might say, "Detroit 5 miles," or "Los Angeles ⇒." In this same way, all signs and miracles from God point straight to Jesus. He's the final destination, the One Who gave everything up for us and Whose love has no limits. The focus is not the gifts or the fruits of the Holy Spirit, but the Giver of the gifts and the fruits, which is Jesus! Our focus must never waver from Him!

THE INTENSIVE CARE UNIT

This is the story of Stiven, a small child of only four years of age who attended the children's center we directed, and who lived on the fourth floor of a nearby slum building. One day while playing, his toy flew out the window onto a ledge below. As he climbed out the window to retrieve the toy, he somehow lost his balance, tumbled, and fell onto the hard concrete street four stories below! Unconscious and bleeding, he was rushed to the hospital with a huge open gash on his forehead.

STIVEN'S GRIM PROGNOSIS

Later that day, his mom called our center in a panic. Stiven was in a coma and the doctors reported that in the unlikely event of his waking up, he would be a paraplegic at best, unable to use his arms and legs. At worst, he would be in a vegetative state for the rest of his life. I knew this family had struggled all their lives just to get by, and now this? It was too much! Compassion rose in me for this distraught mother and her young boy.

Although in human terms this seemed an impossible situation, I had to believe it wasn't impossible for God to heal Stiven. A few of our staff and volunteers who had faith for healing went to the hospital to pray for little Stiven and arrived at the Intensive Care Unit (ICU) floor where only the most critically ill patients go. Hanging in the balance between life and death, these patients are often on life support like Stiven, who was bandaged from head to toe, had severe brain trauma, and was hooked up to a ventilator.

SPEAKING LIFE

I approached the unconscious child, touched his hand, and declared healing in Jesus' name. The others also prayed, and although we could see no immediate signs of improvement, we believed God would do something miraculous. We returned to the waiting room where we counseled and prayed for Stiven's mother. We all agreed to speak life over her son and encouraged her to expect something wonderful to happen.

A few days later, Stiven's mother rushed into the center, eyes lit up with hope. Despite the grim prognosis they had been given, Stiven had defied all odds and come out of his coma! Contrary to what the doctors had said would happen, he was now breathing without a ventilator, talking, and showing normal cognitive function. He could also move his arms and legs and showed no signs of nerve damage!

Stiven's doctors and nurses were astonished at his unbelievable recovery. However, his healing was not the most incredible miracle to happen. A few days later, his mother received an unexpected call from the ICU nurses, who were quite curious to find out exactly who had come in to pray for little Stiven that day.

THE OTHER PATIENTS

When the mother asked why they wanted to know, the nurses explained that it wasn't only little Stiven who had been healed that day. *Every single patient who was dying in the ICU had quickly recovered*! The nurses realized this was not a coincidence, for it had never before happened. They knew beyond any doubt that the prayers that day had healed all the ICU patients!

> *Compassion is love in action, allowing you to carry God's presence into circumstances that seem impossible.*

We were amazed at how much greater God's plans were than ours that day. Just a simple act of faith and obedience brought about one of the most amazing miracles we've ever seen. We'd wanted little Stiven to be healed, but God wanted the entire ICU ward to be healed!

Compassion is *love in action*, allowing you to carry God's presence into circumstances that seem impossible. This is a perfect setup for God to partner with you to bring the manifestation of His Heavenly Kingdom wherever you go.

HE WILL LIVE AND NOT DIE!

Stiven's story is miraculous and inspiring, giving us the faith and motivation to get out of our comfort zones and pray for others. However, God did not stop with Stiven, but also performed a surprising miracle in the life of *another* child at the center!

As I was walking into church one Sunday morning, a hysterical woman came in behind me, her eyes red and wet with tears. She was wailing, "My son is going to die! He's going to die!" I sat her in a chair and asked what had happened.

Crying and gasping for breath, she responded that the night before, her three-year-old son had walked out into the street and been run over by a motorcycle racing past their house. Rushed to the hospital with severe brain trauma, he was now in a coma. The doctors couldn't do anything else for him and determined he would most likely die. The mother continued sobbing and wailing, "He's going to die! He's going to die!"

Taking her hand and looking in her eyes, I said, "You need to stop saying these words *right now*! I will go to the hospital and pray for him today, but first you need to stop declaring death over your son! Declare life over him. Repeat after me, 'He will live and not die.'" As she repeated the phrase, I agreed with her in prayer that her son would live. I then realized that she was not only a member of the church, but that her son also attended the children's center we directed.

TWO GUARDED CHECKPOINTS

Unaware that there are certain hours during the day in which visitors are allowed into the ICU, I arrived at the hospital during a time in which not even family members could enter. I told the first checkpoint guard I was there to see the little boy, and he let me through with no questions. When I approached the officer who was guarding the ICU floor, he informed me that visitors were not allowed at this time. I replied that the guard at the entrance had let me in, and I was there to pray for the boy.

He seemed surprised and asked how I knew the boy. I replied that I was the family's pastor. He looked me up and down, and after a slight hesitation, allowed me through the door. Going to the nurses' station, I told them I was there to pray for the boy. Without question, they gave me instructions to wash my hands up to my elbows, put on a smock, face mask, and hair net, and wait to be taken into the room.

I did as instructed, and soon afterward a nurse approached me, surprised to see a visitor during non-visiting hours. Recognizing that I had made it through two guarded checkpoints and the nurses' station, she asked, dumbfounded, "*Who are you?*"

I replied, "I'm the boy's pastor and a friend of the family." She nodded, still surprised, and led me to the boy's room. Until that point, it hadn't occurred to me that any of this was out of the ordinary. It was as if God had opened all the doors, giving me a VIP pass right to the side of this dying boy. The nurse stayed and watched as I prayed for a full five minutes, rebuking death and declaring life over this small child. The next day I sent other people to pray for him. By the hand of God, within days the boy made an almost complete recovery, and his mother brought him to the children's center to see us.

I was surprised to see a big patch on his right eye, and his mother explained that he had experienced a miraculous recovery *except for that eye*, which had been blinded by the head injury. As I looked at the boy, something rose in me, and I knew I needed to pray for his eye. I was thinking, *blindness in this eye is not God's plan or design for him.* We prayed in complete faith that God would heal his blindness. We didn't see immediate results right after the prayer, but within a week the miracle manifested and his eye was completely healed. The boy now has perfect vision in both eyes!

WHAT IF THEY'RE NOT HEALED?

Although it's wonderful when the Holy Spirit flows in His gifts of healing through us, what happens when a person *doesn't* get healed? Are our efforts in praying for them worthless? Absolutely not! Our primary goal for that person is always for them to experience the love of God through us.

An example of this stands out in my mind as if it were yesterday. Right before we were sent out as missionaries in 2011, one of our mentors who was a seasoned missionary shared that she was struggling with painful back issues. It was so bad that she had planned a much-needed surgery to relieve her pain.

Jen and I approached her and asked if we and our three young children could pray for healing for her back. She agreed, so all five of us put our hands on her back and prayed in complete faith for total healing in Jesus' name. We declared it just like Jesus did, but didn't see any confirmation of healing in the moment. Nonetheless, she received our earnest prayers with gratitude.

Almost seven years later we ran into her at a missions conference. She was thrilled to see us and sought us out. I was astonished when she said that our prayers for her back many years before had changed her life. Although she hadn't received physical healing and had gone on to have the operation, the prayer had marked her for life. She had never seen such love and faith, and it had drawn her closer to God!

For this reason, we must ensure that everyone we pray for receives the genuine love of God. Healings will cease and all people will eventually die, but true love, which is divine, is everlasting. It calls people to the heart of the Father, then fills their hearts to overflowing. It brings them into the family of God where they can spend everlasting life with Him in Heaven. This is our mission, and it is critical!

FOCUS ON THE HEALER

While serving on a forty-member prayer team with a mission trip years ago, I observed quite the opposite. A stout middle-aged man who displayed a powerful gift of healing had a line of people in front of him waiting to receive prayer. He sat them down, and then raced down the line praying for each one's physical healing.

I noticed that every person was in fact healed. However, as the people were healed, this man said with pride, like a basketball player making shots, "One for one! Two for two! Three for three..." and so on. There's nothing wrong with having fun with God, but this man's focus was on the number of people healed, *not* on the love of the Healer for His children.

If a person gets healed but doesn't receive love, they will end up focusing on the *healing* instead of the *Healer*, who is Jesus. They may think, "Great! I got healed. Next time I'm in pain I know where to come. See 'ya 'til then!" However, if our primary motive is love, when the person gets healed they will respond differently. They will think, "Wow! God healed me! He must love me and care about the details of my life. I want to get to know Him better!" It is the only thing that will produce true and everlasting change.

Love provides a safety net into which both the minister and the receiver can fall, whether or not there is an immediate divine healing. Divine healing is a tool showing the love of the Father, because all divine healing comes out of His loving heart. We can use this tool the way it was intended or not. We can be an extension of His love

> *Love provides a safety net into which both the minister and the receiver can fall, whether or not there is an immediate divine healing.*

so that deep and lasting transformation can occur in the hearts of those to whom we minister, or we can ignore it and focus only on the healing. The decision lies in our hands. Which will we choose?

CONCLUSION

If you were stuck in a pit of sin and selfishness, far from a deep and intimate relationship with God, wouldn't you at least want someone to *try* to talk to you about living an abundant life with a loving God? I definitely would!

I can only remember a few times in which somebody flat-out refused a prayer or a blessing. You might be afraid to step out in faith, but I would argue that you really have little to lose, and *what if* God actually moves and heals someone as you pray or talk to them about His love?

If you haven't prayed for many people before, you may feel foolish or scared the first few times. We all do! Why? Because we are stepping out in faith! If God doesn't show up in some way, we might actually look foolish! Are you willing to take that risk?

Jesus took a much greater risk for your soul and for mine. How foolish did He look to others when they ripped out His beard, hit Him, and made fun of Him by telling Him to prophesy who had hit Him? Jesus didn't give an answer, which made Him look even worse in their eyes. He did all that and more, just because He loved us.

How much of a risk are we willing to take for another person's soul? We will never know what God might do unless we step out in faith and pray for them. Cut yourself some slack. Allow yourself to fail at this a few times. Everyone has to learn by trial and error, so don't expect to be the exception.

As Christians we so often talk about faith, yet rarely extend ourselves to the point at which all we have left is our faith, and at which we trust God with all our being to catch us if we fall. Now is your time to step out in faith!

ACTION CHALLENGE

1. Take a moment and ask God to bring someone to mind who needs prayer for physical healing. Now put your faith to action. Call or visit them and pray for healing in Jesus' name.

2. Ask God where He would like you to go to pray for healing (the mall, the park, etc.). When you arrive, be attentive to find somebody who needs prayer. If you don't see anybody with an obvious need, ask those you meet if they have any pain or sickness and would like prayer.

3. What is one area in which you have been challenged through this chapter? What would your life look like if you were to overcome this challenge? Journal your thoughts.

Chapter Six

GANGS!

---

*"I tell you that in the same way there will be more rejoicing
in heaven over one sinner who repents than over ninety-nine
righteous persons who do not need to repent" (NIV, Luke 15:7).*

Medellín, like other large cities around the world, has a significant problem with gangs. Many of these young people are driven to the streets by broken families or communities destroyed by poverty and corruption. Ironically, these youth often end up falling into the roles of both victim and perpetrator.

In neighborhoods where there is a lack of the rule of law by legal authorities, another rule of law enters to fill that vacuum. Although gangs make their money through illegal means, their rule of law in many neighborhoods does embody a certain value system. For example, they try to prevent robberies to avoid attracting the attention of civil authorities.

There is an unspoken understanding among gang leaders that the raping of women or the sexual abuse of children in their neighborhood is abhorred, and they will obtain justice through the quick and private murder of the offender. They also put willing policemen on their payroll to ensure that their gang stays in control of the neighborhood. Thus, the neighborhood in which a person lives determines who they call if a crime is committed. Sometimes the police are the authority, and in other cases it's the gang leaders.

The young men in these gangs desperately need the love of the Heavenly Father. For the most part, their earthly fathers have failed them, leaving gaping wounds in their hearts. Gang members are some of the most despised people in Medellín, due to the crimes they have committed and the toll it's taken on society. However, God sees them through a different perspective - as redeemable humans who were created in His image.

JONAH AND THE GANGSTER

Meeting with high-level gang leaders is a risky business. There is always the possibility of being caught in the middle of a gun fight in case the police or special forces show up. Although we haven't been focused on ministering to gangs or gang leaders, God has opened these doors for us. This means we must have great dependence on God to move in the supernatural, and also to protect us.

Viki, a preschool student teacher who was new at our center, entered my office one morning and surprised me by asking if I could explain about speaking in tongues. I described how the Bible says that speaking in other languages, either angelic or human, is a gift of the Holy Spirit. It often accompanies the infilling of the Holy Spirit, yet we don't always know for certain if a person is genuinely speaking in tongues or not.

As I was sharing this with her, a sudden realization interrupted my thought process. Like a GPS rerouting to correct the path to a destination, I realized this student teacher had received Jesus within the past few weeks. Wondering if the two events might be connected, I asked why she wanted to know about speaking in tongues.

After hesitating a moment, she responded, "Well, last night I was in my bed praying when I felt a literal wind in my room. My spirit felt like it was bubbling inside me, and then out of my mouth came a prayer language I didn't understand!"

"Wow!" I replied. "You don't need *me* to explain speaking in tongues. *You've experienced it yourself!*" As I probed further, she shared that she'd felt deep peace and an inner connection with God. In that moment I felt the tangible presence of God come over me, and the following words came tumbling out of my mouth.

I said, "You didn't know what you were saying, but I have the interpretation. You were declaring a 'new day' over your home, your husband, and your children. There will be a fresh wind of the Holy Spirit in your house which will transform your husband and family. Your husband will no longer be against the move of God in your life, and he will change his ways and come to God." Little did either of us know how true this word would be, or how soon it would come to pass.

THE KINGS OF THE NEIGHBORHOOD

Later that week our psychologist came into my office and shared an impactful message she'd heard at church about the prophet Jonah. "God sent Jonah to bad kings and they repented," she began. "There are bad kings (gangsters) in this neighborhood and I feel called to go to them to explain about Jesus so they can repent of their sins!" She continued, "Since you have so much love for people, will you come with me?"

"Of course!" I replied, sensing God's hand on this, but also understanding the danger this could bring. While discussing how a meeting of this sort could be accomplished, we discovered that one of our student teachers was married to a top gangster in the neighborhood. It turned out to be Viki, the same student teacher who had come into my office the week before!

At first, her husband resisted the thought of coming in to talk because he wasn't sure he could trust us. After much coaxing, however, he relented and agreed to a meeting. Upon entering the psychologist's office, the tangible peace and presence of God overcame him. As a tumbling ocean wave melts the walls of a well-built sand castle, this presence disarmed his apprehension and fear, breaking down the reinforced walls of resistance against God and His love.

Viki's husband opened up his heart for the first time since he was a boy. Crying and repenting before God, he confessed to having committed terrible crimes. Bewildered at how a perfect God could forgive his filth, his face glimmered with hope as the light of Jesus illuminated the rooms of his heart. Then, having received God's forgiveness, he invited Jesus into his aching heart with joy and relief.

He and Viki came in unannounced the following morning for prayer and then fled the neighborhood with their daughter to an undisclosed location. This was necessary to break from the gang, remove themselves from a life of crime, and start a new life.

The Bible says, "When Paul placed his hands on them, the Holy Spirit came on them, and they spoke in tongues and prophesied" (*NIV*, Acts 19:6). This is what happened to Viki and her family. Although nobody had laid hands on her when she was praying in her room, the Holy Spirit had come on her, and she had spoken in tongues and prophesied. Her prophecy had then come true as God breathed a fresh wind of revival over their family. The past was now forgiven and behind them, and the fresh wind of God had allowed them a fresh start in life!

THE EX-HITMAN'S HOUSE

This same fresh wind of God's Holy Spirit touched my friends Camilo and Fernando, who had both been hitmen for one of the most feared gangs in Medellín. Camilo was changed through a personal encounter with God which turned him into a radical follower of Jesus. Camilo then shared his experience with Fernando who in turn had his own encounter with God, which turned him into a radical follower of Jesus, too! We met both passionate followers of Christ at our local church and became instant friends.

Jen and I had been sensing God's prodding to help poor families by either remodeling or building new homes for those living in dilapidated housing. Fernando lived in a worn-down, mold-infested, ten-by-twelve-foot single-room home that leaked and was damp for days every time it rained. The peeling paint, dangling exposed electrical wires, and humid smell of fermenting mold made this humble abode a horrid place to live. Fixing the roof, plumbing, electrical, and walls would get rid of the mold and make the house much safer.

A generous visiting team helped us fix his house, and although Fernando was very grateful, he didn't seem too surprised that we were there. Months later, I bumped into Fernando on the street in his neighborhood, and he shared something unexpected. He explained, "Four years ago, before you came to Colombia, I had a dream in which God showed me a tall American man in the alleyway near my house. In the dream, God said, 'This man is going to fix up your house.' Tom, that man was you. I saw you in my dream before we even met! That's why I wasn't shocked that you fixed my house."

I was stunned and humbled. Fernando had seen me in a dream and been given details of what I would do for him before we even arrived in Colombia! It's both perplexing and comforting to know that God has our steps planned out long before we have any inkling of what the future will hold. His thoughts and plans for us truly are for our well-being!

I was also impacted by God's great love for Fernando, who had dedicated his life to reaching out to the gangs in his neighborhood, a dangerous and tiring job with little help from others. By improving Fernando's house, we were able to support the amazing work he was doing in the neighborhood, thus building into his ministry and helping him to reach more gang leaders for Christ.

A "DANIEL" MOMENT

The Lord continued opening doors for us to reach the gangs, even key leaders of a notorious gang in this same hard-hit neighborhood high in the mountains outside of Medellín. These gang leaders invited us to their meetings to pray for them, and we were able to speak into their lives and counsel them. God moved in supernatural ways every time we met with this group of men, confirming His presence and His great love for them.

During one of our Missions Intensive schools, I shared the testimony about Fernando's dream with the students, and then prayed that God would multiply this testimony in their lives. The next day, we sent small groups of our Missions Intensive students to visit the homes of these key gang leaders and members, to pray for them and their families. One particular group arrived at a home and prayed for the gang leader's mother, who received a significant physical healing. As they were about to leave, the gang leader came stumbling out of a bedroom, shaken from having just woken up from a terrible nightmare.

Perplexed and frightened, he began to explain in Spanish about his terrifying dream. Before he could get more than a few words out, a student leader named John who understood no Spanish at all interrupted him. With eyes lit up as if he had just seen a vision, John blurted out, "Wait...wait...right now God told me this young man has just woken from a terrible dream. God showed me the dream and explained to me what it means!"

All eyes were on John as he explained how in his dream he had watched the young man fall from a cliff. Hitting his head on the rocks below, blood was gushing out of his left ear. Amazed, the gang member confirmed that these were the very details of his dream! God then gave John the interpretation of the dream, which was that the young man's life was in grave and immediate danger. God was giving him a chance to accept Jesus and follow Him before it was too late.

The gang leader was astounded and continued, "Something else happened in the dream. God spoke to me, and said, 'Some people from a different country will come to your house today. You must listen to them, for everything they say is the truth.'" A wave of hope, faith, and the presence of God filled the room like a smoky, pleasant incense. The students, in shock at this divine setup, led this young man to accept Jesus, and he was then delivered from demons. Afterward, his entire countenance changed from one of fear to one of peace, joy, and gratitude.

This was a true "Daniel" moment, as if the team had stepped into a Bible story with themselves as the key characters. In the book of Daniel, there's a story in which King Nebuchadnezzar had a dream. He called in his advisors and told them they must not only interpret his dream, but *first tell him what it was he dreamt*! None could do it, and the king threatened to execute all the Babylonian wise men, including Daniel and his friends, if nobody could do this impossible thing.

God delights in using regular people to be part of something extraordinary!

Daniel asked God to reveal to him the dream and its meaning. He then received from God both the details of King Nebuchadnezzar's dream and also its interpretation. This saved Daniel's life, and brought him honor and authority in that kingdom. This happened in our story, too, as John is now honored among the gang members and given authority to speak into their lives, leading them ever closer toward the righteousness of God. God delights in using regular people to be part of something extraordinary!

CHRISTIANS AND CRIMINALS

At some point in our gang ministry, one of the leaders mentioned that he was trying to build a house for his wife and son because he didn't expect to live long and wanted to make sure they had a place to live once he was killed. Camilo and I came up with a crazy idea to help this gang leader build his house. We would partner with some key people and organizations to help fund the project, along with an American mission team which would help with the construction.

The American team would work together with local Christians and also gang members to build the house. We would not ask the gang members to come to church or do anything in return for our help. Since their money is "dirty," having been gained through illicit means, we would buy the building materials with honest, hard-earned money, in this way hoping to bring a blessing over this project and the gang.

Everyone despises these gang members because of the atrocities they have committed. They are outcasts and their lives are worth very little in society, but we wanted to send them a different message. We Christians would offer love instead of condemnation, and we would ask for nothing in return. The kindness of God shown through us would be the best tool to bring them to repentance.

I told the leader whose house we would build that we wanted all of his gang members to work alongside us. He agreed, and as honest Christians and ruthless killers worked together side-by-side, an amazing thing happened. These gang members began asking for prayer! I'd instructed our team to love these guys to life, and many in the gang received prayer, resulting in salvations, physical healing, and deliverance. It was a beautiful time of *demonstrating* what the love of Jesus looks like when we take risks to love our neighbor.

Many of these criminals cannot go to church because they are hiding from the police or other gangs. They wouldn't be accepted in most churches anyway! The only way for them to know Jesus is for *us* to go to *them*. Our going sends the mission-critical message that they are important and valued by the loving Heavenly Father. God is not mad at them. They already know they are sinners, but the kindness of God calls them to repentance and forgiveness, and then invites them to change their ways and run into His loving arms.

CONCLUSION

Every one of us is given the opportunity to reach out to others. Opportunities in our context may look a little different from yours. You don't have to do the same things we do. However, you *do* need to walk through the doors God opens, for on the other side are divine appointments He has set up for you to carry out.

In the stories we've just shared, the open doors always came through relationships. We were attentive to the relationships we already had, listening to the voice of God and also to the suggestions of those around us. Through the psychologist and student teacher, a local gang leader and his family were transformed by Christ. It was through my relationship with Fernando and recognizing a need in his life that we were able to fix up his house and support his ministry.

It was out of love for the Missions Intensive students that I shared Fernando's dream, wanting it to inspire faith and multiply in their lives. My friendship with Fernando and Camilo allowed us access to the neighborhood and gang leaders. We didn't force any of these things to happen. They were just a natural result of loving the people in our lives, and of listening to and obeying the voice of God.

As you love those around you and walk through the doors of opportunity God provides, you will see Him work through you in surprising ways. Your stories will differ from ours, and that's good! You will have your own amazing stories of God's supernatural intervention in your life and the lives of others. Allow our

> *As you love those around you and walk through the doors of opportunity God provides, you will see Him work through you in surprising ways.*

stories to multiply in you. Give God access to every part of your life and believe that He will use you in amazing ways. *Let your faith arise*!

ACTION CHALLENGE

1. Think about the relationships and friendships you already have. Ask God to open doors of blessing to others through these relationships.
2. Talk to one or more of your faith-filled friends, and dream about how you can work together to reach others with the love of Jesus. Once you come up with some ideas, put them into action. Don't worry about the outcome. God will take care of that!
3. Write about your dreams and experiences in your journal.

Chapter Seven

A GUN TO CONQUER FEAR?

> *"There is no fear in love. But perfect love drives out fear, because fear has to do with punishment. The one who fears is not made perfect in love" (NIV, 1 John 4:18).*

Imagine moving to a country in which everything is unfamiliar. You're unsure of how to behave within the culture, and you are missing many non-verbal communication cues. On top of this, you have only a modest command of the language. You have just entered into an environment in which you now need to throw out most of the tools you normally use to interact with people. Stripped of almost everything that used to work in your home culture, you are perplexed by even very simple things to which you've never before given a second thought. To sum it up, everyone else seems to know what's going on, yet you are pretty much clueless.

DISPLACING FEAR

Now imagine that you've been given a ministry and a team of amazing people to lead. How would you feel? Well, if you're like my wife and me, you would feel somewhat insecure and helpless in this unfamiliar environment. You might even think, "What in the world do *I* have to offer here?" This is how we felt moving to Colombia as new missionaries. We were living and working among people who knew the language, culture, and communication styles better than we did, and they even dressed better than us! I figured they could even run the ministry better. Why on Earth had God called *us* to this place?

WHAT DO WE HAVE TO OFFER?

Throughout our many years of preparation to become missionaries, I had often asked Father God what I had to offer in Colombia that would make an impact. As hard as I tried, I couldn't imagine His answer, because to the best of my ability I couldn't even come up with a suitable response to my own question. When He answered, His response was simple. He said in a soft and confident voice, "You can love them. You may think you have nothing to offer, yet your primary mission in Colombia is to love."

That was encouraging! I realized that no matter how insecure or inferior I felt on the inside, I could still offer love to others. What does love look like? When talking to someone, love takes a genuine interest in them and what they care about. It looks them in their eyes and gives them full attention, expressing genuine affection in a way that communicates the other person is important. Love puts aside a personal agenda, coming alongside the other person in a helpful way. It makes others feel at ease, and it's something we can always do no matter where we are or with whom. Love never fails!

We did this simple thing that God asked of us, choosing to be intentional about every interaction. Although due to our language deficit we may not have understood everything others were saying, we focused on how we could best express love to the one in front of us.

Sometimes it was as simple as giving a genuine hug or smile, or just listening to them. As we focused on loving those around us, an interesting thing happened. Other thoughts of insecurity, inferiority, and fear now had no place to land in our minds! We were so focused on loving others in every interaction and conversation that we couldn't think about our own issues at the same time. As we put our attention on love, it displaced all of the fear and insecurity!

After the negative, pestering, insecure thoughts disappeared, God began to show us why we, in particular, were a perfect fit for this new position, place, and culture. One day while in prayer, I asked, "Why me, God? These people are so smart and talented! They're capable of running this place just as well as I can."

Breaking the silence, the Lord spoke. His words resonated within my heart the same way guitar strings resonate when played in unison. He said, "Tom, I've sent you to multiply your missionary heart in the hearts of these staff members, children, and families, and to impart the Father's love I've given you!" I was undone by the incredible wisdom, grace, and mercy of a Father who knows us better than we even know ourselves.

HEALTHY FAMILIES HEAL FAMILIES

Our ministry serves a population decimated by the lack of the father's love. There is an almost universal lack of true paternity, as most of the fathers have neglected their families and commitments. These men have fallen into drugs, promiscuity, homelessness, and violence. Many are in prison or dead, leaving their families in utter crisis.

The Lord had given me His Father's heart so I could help restore what was lacking in the city. He didn't send me alone, but with my entire family. Imagine His wisdom in sending a healthy family to heal families! He intended to use our healthy marriage and family as an example and testimony of His love which would encourage and help others. Although our family is far from perfect, we have received so much healing that we can now point others in the right direction, helping them to find God's plan amid their chaos.

Most new missionaries who come to partner with us go through a similar phase of insecurity, inferiority, and fear. After all, the Colombians are amazing! Our advice to new missionaries is to keep it simple and love from your heart those with whom you come into contact. Aim to change the world one person at a time.

Fear and insecurity are a struggle for almost every person on the planet. As humans, we tend to compare ourselves to others, focusing on what they *have* that we *don't*. This causes a downward spiral that can spin us out of control. Comparing our weaknesses to other people's strengths is never wise. God has created us to be different from each other. Instead of focusing on our differences, let's focus on the one thing every person on Earth has in common - everyone desires to be loved.

God has commanded and entrusted us to share His love with others. This is more practical than theological. As we look at others through eyes of pure love instead of comparison, insecurity, inferiority, and fear, there's no space to build up our defenses. At the same time, this pure love breaks down the defenses in the one in front of us. It conquers fear by displacement. In other words, it fills in the area fear used to occupy, leaving no room for it to reenter.

> *As we look at others through eyes of pure love instead of comparison, insecurity, inferiority, and fear, there's no space to build up our defenses.*

THE GUN

While God was preparing us and confirming our call to Colombia in many encouraging and miraculous ways, Jen spoke at a women's conference which I wanted to attend. A well-known female speaker was giving the key message, and I sensed this was what I needed to hear for the next season of my journey. I'm not sure if this has happened to any of you other men out there. You hear of an amazing, Godly speaker that you'd love to hear, but then discover she's speaking at a women's conference...and you can't go!

The day after the conference, Jen and I flew to Texas for training. During the flight I asked Jen to transmit what she'd experienced at the women's event, and she gave me a detailed summary of what she'd learned. Jen had my complete attention as she spoke. Something both Jen and I understood but others may not have seen is that I had struggled with doubt, fear, and anxiety throughout much of my young adulthood. Although I dreamed of doing exceptional things for the Lord, a negative voice would always come into my head, crowding out the dream and causing me to doubt myself.

As Jen talked, she explained the novel concept of the "Philippians 4 Gun" which the speaker had discussed. It goes something like this: you memorize Philippians 4:4-9, and as habitual negative thoughts come into your mind, you make an imaginary gun with your hand, and use each life-giving verse as a bullet to shoot the negative thought out of your mind. With every shot, you visualize the life-giving verses and either say them out loud or recite them in your mind. After that, you commit to obeying those verses.

OUR FOCUS

What do these verses say that make them so powerful? They say, "Rejoice in the Lord always. I will say it again: Rejoice! Let your gentleness be evident to all. The Lord is near. Do not be anxious about anything, but in every situation, by prayer and petition, with thanksgiving, present your requests to God. And the peace of God, which transcends all understanding, will guard your hearts and your minds in Christ Jesus. Finally, brothers and sisters, whatever is true, whatever is noble, whatever is right, whatever is pure, whatever is lovely, whatever is admirable—if anything is excellent or praiseworthy—think about such things. Whatever you have learned or received or heard from me, or seen in me—put it into practice. And the God of peace will be with you" (*NIV*, Philippians 4:4-9).

If a thought doesn't fit within the requirements of these verses, *we must annihilate it*. Philippians 4:4-7 tells us what to do with anxious, negative thoughts, while Philippians 4:8-9 tells us what to fill our minds with instead. Paul first commands us to rejoice, showing that rejoicing is more of a choice than a reaction. "Rejoice in the Lord always. I will say it again: Rejoice" (*NIV*, Philippians 4:4)!

Paul reminds us to be gentle in all situations. "Let your gentleness be evident to all. The Lord is near" (*NIV*, Philippians 4:5). He assures us God is at our side, and then gives us a step-by-step plan of what to do if we feel anxious. "Do not be anxious about anything, but in every situation, by prayer and petition, with thanksgiving, present your requests to God" (*NIV*, Philippians 4:6). We are to present every situation to God, in thanksgiving and without grumbling or complaining. We are to put all of our worrisome and negative thoughts in God's hands, trusting that He will take them from us. This is where the gratefulness and thanksgiving come in!

What is the result? It says, "And the peace of God, which transcends all understanding, will guard your hearts and your minds in Christ Jesus" (*NIV*, Philippians 4:7). The result is peace! What wonderful news!

WHOSE THOUGHTS ARE THEY?

The concept that I had the power to reject any thought and take control of my thought life was novel to me. Just because a thought came into my mind didn't mean I had to entertain it or accept it! It didn't mean the thought had come from me, either.

What was happening? Well, here was my problem. Without realizing it, I had allowed a lot of negative thinking to occupy my mind. We all have people in our lives who say negative things to us, whether teachers, brothers or sisters, parents, friends, enemies, or even messages from the media. I'd gone well beyond the simple step of giving these messages a place in my mind. I'd even added some negative thoughts of my own! I would dwell on thoughts like, "People don't like me. I will not be successful in life. I'm not good enough."

On top of this came other thoughts that weren't mine at all but were projected at me from the enemy. To make it even more confusing, I didn't know which thoughts were which, because for so many years I had taken ownership of them all! Have you ever heard the phrase, "You are what you eat?" The same is true of our thought life. You are what you think!

Since I struggled with inadequacy, fear, and insecurity in my thought life, it was difficult for me to make any decision on my own and be confident about it. I have since learned that every accusatory thought is from the accuser, while every inspiring, positive, life-giving thought is from our Friend and Advocate, the Holy Spirit.

PULLING OUT THE GUN

If you're like me, when you first start this process you may pull out your gun every few minutes. That was revealing! After Jen shared the teaching with me, I put it into practice right away. It may sound silly to form your hand and fingers into a pretend gun like you did when you were a kid, to point it at yourself, say a loud "bang," and then recite Scripture out loud or in your head, but that's what I did.

I pulled out my gun every few minutes, sometimes grabbing an "Uzi" because the lies the enemy was pumping into my mind were so large and negative that they required more firepower. I recall Jen looking over at me in amazement as I pulled out my gun dozens of times on that brief flight. We were both surprised at the vast number and frequency of negative thoughts I experienced.

These thoughts were so pervasive that I spent the following few days "shooting" myself several times each minute. I was aggressive about it, because I realized an enormous part of my mind had been hijacked, and I wanted it back. The results were stunning! The negative thoughts slowed down, and within a week much of the negative thought storm had stopped. Within two weeks I had gained control over my thought life.

As I carried out the instructions given in Philippians 4, peace that I couldn't understand came into my life and started to protect my heart and mind from negative thoughts, just as the Bible says: "And the peace of God, which transcends all understanding, will guard your hearts and your minds in Christ Jesus" (*NIV*, Philippians 4:7). That's how the gun works. As you "shoot" the negative thoughts and lies coming from the enemy, you stop "feeding" them and begin to replace the enemy's lies with God's truths. This results in the kind of peace that passes all understanding.

> *It's not enough to commit to stop thinking negative thoughts. You have to take action by displacing the negative thoughts with the positive, life-giving Word of God!*

CONCLUSION

Think about how your life might change if several times each minute you viewed, read, or meditated on Philippians 4:4-9. Begin by saturating your mind with good, excellent, and praiseworthy thoughts. It's not enough to commit to stop thinking negative thoughts. You have to take action by displacing the negative thoughts with the positive, life-giving Word of God!

ACTION CHALLENGE

1. What does your thought life consist of during an average day? What percentage of your thoughts are negative? Would you like to change that percentage? Write your answers in your journal.

2. Write out Philippians 4:4-9 on a piece of paper or in your phone and keep it with you. Every time a negative thought comes to your mind, pull out your Philippians 4 gun and "shoot" it. Then read Philippians 4, speaking these life-giving words over yourself and your mind. Do this until the habitual negative thoughts have been replaced by positive, life-giving thoughts.

3. Journal during this process to help you identify your habits and the difference Philippians 4:4-9 is making in your thought life.

Chapter Eight

"MR. LOVE"

*"Be completely humble and gentle; be patient, bearing
with one another in love" (NIV, Ephesians 4:2).*

Has it ever occurred to you that love and humility are two sides of the same coin? This is because genuine love always causes us to humble ourselves before our Lord and King. We find a great definition of humility in Philippians, where Paul writes, "Do nothing out of selfish ambition or vain conceit. Rather, in humility *value others above yourselves* [emphasis added], not looking to your own interests but each of you to the interests of the others" (*NIV*, Philippians 2:3-4).

NO ONE CAN GO LOWER

While serving as one of twelve associate pastors at a local megachurch in Medellín, I often spoke to large audiences from the platform. Each time I ministered, I would take a moment to pray for God's presence to be with me before stepping onto the stage. On one particular occasion, I was just about to walk onto the platform to give a salvation message when I had an unexpected and startling vision of Jesus.

In the vision I was already on the platform talking to the people, and Jesus was *inside* the floor on which I walked, as if covered by glass. I could see Him lying face up looking at me from beneath a transparent window of glass, yet I couldn't touch Him. A crown of thorns was on His head, and blood covered His shirtless body. As strange as it sounds, it seemed as though I were *walking on Jesus*!

I was horrified. If anybody should be on top doing the walking, it should be Jesus, and *I* should be the one lying on the ground! I was so distraught by the vision and how wrong it was that I slid to the ground, trying in vain to get lower than He was. I cried out, "No, Jesus! This isn't right! I'm not worthy to be walking here. Please let me go lower!" In the vision, I was trying to get *into* the floor, but it was impossible for me to get any lower. I cried out in desperation, "Why? This doesn't make sense. I *will not* walk on You like this!"

Then I heard God the Father answer, "My Son has humbled Himself and made Himself more lowly than anyone else. You cannot have greater humility or make yourself go lower than He has. He paid the price for your dignity and worthiness, so if you are confident that He took your sin and filth away and made you a worthy son, you'll walk where He tells you to walk, even if it looks like this. Just remember, His humility put you here, giving you the power and love to minister, and only your pride can take that away. You must minister in humility!"

As I tried to pull myself together after this encounter and make it up the stairs to the platform, the fear and awe of the Lord filled me. Although He enabled me to minister well, it was a great relief to get down afterwards. He had called me a dignified and worthy son, yet there was a clear understanding that He is the All-powerful, Almighty God and I am His small creation.

AUTHORITY AND HUMILITY

Jesus opens the door for us to seek humility and then shows us how to walk in it. He urges, "Take my yoke upon you. Let me teach you, because I am humble and gentle at heart, and you will find rest for your souls" (*NLT*, Matthew 11:29).

Paul says we must "have the same attitude as Christ Jesus" (*NLT*, Philippians 2:5). He then describes what that means. Have you ever heard or read the Bible verse that talks about how every knee will bow to Jesus and every tongue will confess that He is Lord? This is one of my favorite verses! Why is Jesus given such great honor? What could He have done to deserve it?

Paul gives us the answer in Philippians when he tells us, "Though he was God, he did not think of equality with God as something to cling to. Instead, he gave up his divine privileges; he took the humble position of a slave and was born as a human being. When he appeared in human form, he *humbled himself* [emphasis added] in obedience to God and died a criminal's death on a cross. *Therefore,* [emphasis added] God elevated him to the place of highest honor and gave him the name above all other names, that at the name of Jesus every knee should bow, in heaven and on earth and under the earth, and every tongue declare that Jesus Christ is Lord, to the glory of God the Father" (*NLT*, Philippians 2:6-11).

> *He loves and values us so much that He paid the ultimate price to save us from our sin.*

Did you catch that? Jesus receives this honor as a *result* of His humility. Do you know what drove Jesus to humble Himself so much? His *love* for you and me is what drove Him to such depths of humility. He loves and values us so much that He paid the ultimate price to save us from our sin. He considers us worth dying for! That's almost incomprehensible, isn't it?

Since the source of Jesus' great authority comes from His great humility, our authority should also come from a humble willingness to love and serve others. As we spend our lives helping and encouraging others, it will be natural for us to grow in authority and influence.

EATING "HUMBLE PIE"

Often the way we grow in humility is through making mistakes. The bigger the mistake, the greater the chance to humble yourself. One of the most humbling experiences in my entire life had to do with me trying to fix a colossal problem I had created. There are times in life when we wish we could undo something foolish we did or said. This was one of those times!

The children's center was run on a tight budget, and we relied on local universities who sent student teachers to do their six-month internships with us for free. This was essential, as we needed the manpower to take care of so many children.

We developed a relationship with a particular university who agreed to send us a significant number of student teachers one year. Toward the end of that year, their coordinator wanted to do something special to celebrate the end of the year and brought all of the university's sixty-five student teachers to throw a party. They would be in charge of the event, providing games and activities for the two hundred children at our center.

> *Often the way we grow in humility is through making mistakes. The bigger the mistake, the greater the chance to humble yourself.*

DOING THINGS HIS WAY

When the day of the event came, the student teachers arrived accompanied by three professors. At some point, one of these professors wanted to extend an activity, which would result in having to move lunchtime later for some of the children. I now realize the professor did not understand the exact precision and coordination required to feed two hundred children from one compact kitchen while adhering to the strict schedule stipulated by the regulating government authorities. Even a ten-minute change in the schedule could have disastrous consequences if the Health Department were to show up, as they do from time to time.

I was annoyed when he asked for the third time and then insisted on changing the schedule. Harassed by his pushiness and not having one of my finer days, I brought all the professors together and in a harsh manner explained that we could not change the schedule under any circumstances.

It was as if all of my lessons on love and humility went out the window that day, and I didn't speak with love, but with frustration. I didn't try to see the situation from their point of view. Instead, I "set down the law" in no uncertain terms. To make matters worse, it wasn't just the three professors who heard my discourse; a sizable group of student teachers who were seated nearby also heard the tense conversation.

THE REALIZATION

As I arrived at work the next day, I was still trying to justify my attitude with little success. Finally, I had to be honest and admit that I'd made a tremendous mistake. I talked to a few staff members who had witnessed the incident, and they confirmed my suspicions. This was hard to stomach, because "Mr. Love" had just demonstrated in front of professors, student teachers, and his own staff that at times he is not very loving. I realized what had to be done. I needed to go to the university and ask the professors and students to forgive me. Humble Pie is easy to say but hard to eat, and this was the very last thing I wanted to do!

The coordinator was surprised to see me at the university, and I called her out of her class for a moment. Apologizing, I explained that there was no excuse for the way I had behaved the day before, and asked for forgiveness. When she replied, "Come with me. This is something the whole class should hear," my stomach dropped. I would now need to apologize in front of the entire group of students!

Humbling myself before all of those sixty-five students was like resetting a fractured bone without anesthesia. It was the right thing to do, but very painful. I had to explain what I had done, listen to how it affected them, and ask for their forgiveness. The students said they thought I was a likeable guy, but were hurt by the way I had acted. It was a great relief to find they all were willing to forgive me. After that, I went in search of the other professors. Surprised to see me, they also listened to my apology and found room in their hearts to offer forgiveness. Apologizing had been extremely painful, but the right thing to do.

WOULD THEY EVER COME BACK?

This event had occurred at the end of one school year, so the nagging question in my mind at the beginning of the next year was whether the university would still send us their student teachers. I was surprised and relieved to find that they did, and because of this something wonderful happened!

The university sent all sixty-five student teachers to the children's center one day to learn more about our ministry. One of our staff members shared the Gospel with them in a creative way, during which almost all the student teachers began to cry as they felt the tangible presence of God come over them. In tears, they repented for their sins and asked Jesus to come into their hearts.

In the midst of this emotional moment, the coordinator arrived. Looking around the room like a detective at the scene of a crime, she asked with concern why her students were crying. Confident in the move of God in the room, our staff member explained the Gospel to the coordinator in the same manner she had explained it to the others. Toward the middle of the explanation, the peace and love of God settled on her shoulders and the coordinator also broke out in tears under the tangible love of God. She then accepted Jesus into her heart!

Despite the obvious awkwardness of having had to fix the mess I'd created, there is a powerful message in this story. Although the problem came about because of my pride, humility opened the door for sixty-five university students and their coordinator to receive Jesus. Growing in humility can be painful, but it's what Jesus calls us to do, and it brings Heavenly rewards.

THE DAY I LOST LOVE

A few months before the situation with the university professor took place, I felt God's tremendous grace of love lift off of me one morning. Before that, I'd had an almost constant genuine love for just about everyone I saw. This was a grace I did not earn and do not deserve, yet I believe it was given to help fulfill our unique calling. I also believe we are not alone in this, but that our generous God gives this special grace of love to many of His children.

This love would prompt me to smile and hug others, and to encourage and laugh with them. I would forget my agenda and love those in my path with a genuine, uncomplicated, and childlike love. More often than not God would do some special miracle for them.

That morning, however, I found that I had much less energy and love for other people. I still knew I should hug them, and I did, but what I wanted to do was run the other way! How was I going to survive my strenuous job if I wasn't feeling genuine love for those around me?

I brought it up with Papa God, and He assured me He had lifted this grace for just a season to teach me about its origin. He explained that the grace of love I'd been experiencing and enjoying were His, and that He uses it to love others through me. Even the smiles I got from others belonged not to me, but to Him!

I asked, seeking clarification, "So those smiles were never meant for me?"

He replied, "I am sufficient for you. Every word from My mouth is yours."

Bible verses and transformational words the Lord had spoken to me in our personal conversations trickled into my mind. In my head were echoing the words, "You are my Son, whom I love; with you I am well pleased" (*NIV*, Mark 1:11). In the Bible, the Father spoke these words to Jesus, but I believe He also speaks them over all His children.

I realized that since the Word of God is Jesus Himself, Jesus is my sufficiency. I need to feed on Him and every Word that comes from the mouth of God, showing my trust that He is all I need by not looking elsewhere. The smiles and accolades of people are mere crumbs compared to the pure feast of joy that my Father has set before me through His Word.

CRITICISM AND PRAISE

In time, the grace of His love came back to me. However, it was during this time in which the grace of His love had lifted that I not only grew in humility but also learned how to receive both criticism and praise.

How we see and define ourselves affects how we walk out humility in our lives. If we are too concerned about our reputation or what others may think of us, we won't be empowered to follow the leading of the Holy Spirit wherever He goes. Humility requires that we not be moved by what others think or say about us, whether positive or negative.

We must allow the continual flow of encouraging and loving words from Father God to wash over us and cleanse us every minute of the day. Our identity must be secure in who He says we are. We cannot allow ourselves to be exhilarated by the praises of others, nor shaken by inappropriate or misplaced criticism. Our confidence must come from who we are in Christ Jesus. If we walk in genuine humility, we are free to love ourselves and others, regardless of whether they offer us praise or criticism. That's liberating!

THE HEART MOTIVE

Genuine humility means that our purpose, confidence, and value are found in God alone. God doesn't just *observe* what we're doing throughout our day. He perceives and cares about the motivations of our hearts, the reasons *why* we do what we do. We may act or speak in positive ways, but it is by the intentions of our hearts that we are judged. We must not only do the right thing but do it for the right reasons!

Paul's letter to the Corinthians gives us one of the most beautiful expositions ever spoken about the importance of love. He reminds us, "If I give all I possess to the poor and give over my body to hardship that I may boast, but do not have love, I gain nothing" (*NIV*, 1 Corinthians 13:3). He's saying that I can give everything I have to the poor, but if my heart motivation is not love, *my sacrifice is worthless*. Even if I give my *life* for something or someone, if the intention of my heart is not motivated by love, I gain nothing. It would be quite a loss to give your life up for nothing, yet many people live their entire lives without a heart motivated by love.

CONCLUSION

Godly humility doesn't mean we should undervalue the gifts God has given us. The key is to remember they are on loan to us from God. This is the very point the Apostle Paul makes in Ephesians: "Although I am less than the least of all of God's people, this grace was given me: to preach to the gentiles the boundless riches of Christ" (*NIV*, Ephesians 3:8). Paul acknowledges his lowly state, yet also recognizes the role and mission given him, along with the grace given to fulfill it.

Examine your life and how you react to unexpected negative situations. Do you react or overreact in ways that reveal patterns of pride? Imagine being open and vulnerable before God, and Him wrapping His arms around you in full acceptance. In His arms all of your defenses, doubts, and apprehensions float away. You are cleansed and filled from the inside out by His love. Imagine arriving at a point at which all of your heart motivations are pure, and at which you know who you are and who you were made to be in Jesus. At this point you are no longer swayed by praise or criticism. This is where God is leading you!

ACTION CHALLENGE

1. Like me, have you struggled with pride? Take a moment and give this struggle to Papa God. Ask Him to work on your character, teaching you how to have genuine humility. Jesus has already paid the price for this, whether or not you believe you deserve it.
2. Quiet your mind and ask God to tell you what you mean to Him. Write this answer in your journal. Allow Him to speak life over you every day!

Chapter Nine

AGAINST ALL ODDS

"I am in them and you are in me. May they experience such
perfect unity that the world will know that you sent me and
that you love them as much as you love me" (NIV, John 17:23).

Many studies have been conducted on child development correlating mothers and their influence on children. Only in the last few decades have experts within the field of psychology studied the influence of fathers in the lives of their children, and the findings are astounding. These studies have found something surprising - the influence of fathers is even greater than that of mothers!

MY FATHER WOUND

I was fortunate enough to grow up in a home in which I lived with both of my parents. Although they were great parents, they were far from perfect. My father was a regional salesman who traveled from Monday through Friday every week. On weekends he did business planning and yard work. I loved and cherished the times I spent with him, but they were few.

At an early age, I often felt an unidentifiable lonely feeling in the pit of my stomach. I had a cherished stuffed animal named Teddy, and every day after school I would see him on my bed and feel a deep ache in my stomach because he'd been alone all day. Feeling his loneliness, I suffered terrible guilt and sadness for not having been there for him. I didn't realize that I was feeling my own loneliness and longing to spend time with my father. Not able to express what I was feeling, I'd projected it onto my Teddy.

My father's father had been a heavy drinker and a workaholic. He'd pursued extramarital relationships and could not form positive connections with his children. Many in the community despised him, bringing shame and disgrace to his family.

I now see how far my father had come as a husband and parent, overcoming much of what he had suffered under my grandfather. I know he tried his hardest to be the best father possible, and he did much better than his own dad had done. However, he did not have many of the emotional tools needed. He was almost always distant and seemed more interested in a myriad of things other than me and my heart. Even as an adult, being around him still stirred up the loneliness that had been there my entire life.

THE GAME OF CATCH THAT NEVER HAPPENED

One Saturday afternoon when I was ten years old, I thought it would be a wonderful idea to play catch with my dad. Seeing him in the hallway next to the kitchen, I got the baseball and two mitts, and asked if he would play ball with me. He said "No," because he wanted to do other things.

I begged, "Dad, *please* play with me. It will just be for a few minutes."

My mom heard us from the kitchen and said in a loud voice, "Gordon, play catch with your son."

"No!" he replied with firmness in his voice.

"Go do it!" she yelled back at him.

"I don't want to!" he shouted back.

Then she came out of the kitchen into the hall and started yelling, "Play catch with your son! He needs you! He needs his father to play catch with him!"

He yelled back, angry now, "*NO! I'M NOT PLAYING CATCH!*" I watched in horror at the situation I had caused, as they continued to fight and yell at each other.

In that moment my heart shattered, and a deep, painful sadness entered. Stepping away, I said, "No, no, it's okay. Please don't yell. I don't want to play catch anymore. It's okay." However, I wasn't okay, and that was the last time I ever asked my father to play catch with me.

Wanting to disappear forever, I went to my room wondering why my own father didn't even like me or want to be with me. What harm was there in playing catch for ten minutes? Why did he object in such a stubborn way? It was as if I held no value in his life. My heart was cracked and hurt, and it would be years before my damaged heart would be restored.

HURTING AND DESPERATE

During high school my father sat in front of the television every night. Many times I tried to get his attention, but it was like seeing something desirable on the other side of a glass wall, yet never being able to attain it. After years of seeing him give more attention to the television than to me, I felt such incredible anger that I decided to destroy the television right in front of my father using an ax he had in the garage. I'm not sure what stopped me from carrying out the plan, but the desire to do this showed how much I was hurting and desperate for a connection with him.

In college I learned how to drink. I thought, *Now I can take my dad out so we can talk and have fun like I do with my college buddies.* One evening, I invited him out to a bar, and to my surprise he agreed to go.

I had waited so long and was in expectant anticipation of being able to finally connect with him, man to man.

When the evening came, I watched in disbelief as he talked to everybody else in that bar except for me. I tried my best to get his attention, but it just didn't work. He was in his own world, engaging everyone with questions and comments the way I wanted him to do to me. Perplexed and devastated, I felt my already damaged heart harden even more. Realizing there was nothing in my power that would bring about a closer relationship with my dad, I pulled away from him in my heart and didn't try to connect with him again. It was too painful.

A FATHER'S IMPACT

Researching the impact fathers have on their children, I realized that all the risky behaviors I had engaged in during college were connected to the father wound in my heart. However, as I'd turned my heart toward my Heavenly Father to heal and fill it with His love, I was drawn less and less to those risky behaviors.

I had to trust and depend on Him *by faith* to fill in all the gaps and holes in my heart that my earthly father couldn't fill. I had to exercise childlike faith to believe what God says in the Bible about His love for me and His promises for my future. It took time sitting in His presence to combat the lies I'd believed for so long, gradually replacing them with God's truths. It also required humility to repent of my sin and judgements against my earthly father.

We can't trust or put our faith in God until we are secure in His love for us. Genuine faith comes from knowing and being filled with God's love. Then, as we experience this love, we are changed from the inside out. Our view of ourselves and our identity change, and we can see God and ourselves in a clearer, more accurate light - the light of truth.

Cassie Carsten's book *The World Needs a Father* (Carstens, 2015)[ii] addresses the worldwide epidemic of the lack of the father's love endured by so many children. Fatherlessness is the root of many world problems such as mass killings, poverty, corruption, and other innumerable heinous crimes committed against humanity.

While the lack of a father is proven to affect children negatively, growing up with a father who lives in the home yet is distant or dysfunctional can also have dramatic negative effects. This is well-documented in Josh McDowell's "Father Factor Portfolio" (McDowell, 2015)[iii], which reflects a quarter-century of meticulous research on the effects of the relationship between fathers and their children, both for good and for bad.

THE GREATEST INFLUENCE

McDowell found that *one single element* has a stronger influence on those under twenty-five years old than anything else. Greater than drug or alcohol addiction, promiscuity, delinquency, and many other negative behaviors, this influence is none other than that of a loving father.

McDowell's research concluded:

- The love of a father is even more influential than that of the mother.[iv]
- Without a loving father in their lives, children have a greater risk of being insecure, hostile, and aggressive.[v]
- Rejection from a father is proven to cause drug and alcohol abuse, addiction, behavior problems, and difficulty in long-term relationships.[vi]
- Children with uninvolved fathers are five times more likely to live in poverty.[vii]
- Children are 68% more likely to smoke, drink, and abuse drugs when they have a poor relationship with their father, even if they live in the same home.[viii]
- Children with absent fathers face almost twice as much abuse.[ix]
- Children in single-parent homes are at:[x]
    o 77% greater risk of being physically abused

o   87% greater risk of being harmed by physical neglect

o   80% greater risk of suffering serious injury as a result of abuse

o   120% greater risk of being endangered by some type of child abuse

FATHERHOOD IN COLOMBIA

These statistics show how damaging the lack of a father can be. We see this in exponential proportions in Colombia, where it's very common for men to father children with multiple women and then disappear from their lives altogether. The following sobering statistics demonstrate in an all too clear way the extent to which the enemy has destroyed families in this beautiful country.

According to the 2015 report of The World Family Map, Colombia has:[xi]

- The highest percentage in the world of children born out of wedlock (84%)
- The highest cohabitation levels in the world (35%)
- The highest percentage in all of South America of children living without both biological parents (11%)

However, in Colombia and other countries the opposite is also true. Where fathers are emotionally and physically present in their children's lives, these children thrive and are less likely to fall into addiction and substance abuse.[xii] As these children become teens, they have reduced teen pregnancy rates and less risky behaviors than do teens who don't benefit from the presence of a loving father in the home.[xiii]

GOOD NEWS

The message is clear: healthy fathers create healthy children. However, many of us did not grow up in homes with emotionally healthy fathers. Many of us grew up in homes where no father was present at all. If a healthy father is so crucial to a child's well-being, how are we to find any hope for ourselves? Is our future doomed with continued suffering from that loss and the wounds it created? I have good news for you. The answer is no! *There is hope!*

I know this seems to go against all of the statistics we just mentioned. However, *what if* the act of receiving Jesus into your heart causes you to become *adopted* by the Heavenly Father? What if He, in turn, fills in all the empty holes your earthly father left in your heart?

What if He could give you a very different and positive experience of having a good and loving Father? Then you would be part of the statistics that talk about children who benefit from good and loving fathers, allowing the negative characteristics due to the influence of an unhealthy or absent father to fall away.

To us, this type of change may seem impossible. However, we aren't children of a human God, but of a supernatural God. I've seen God heal deep wounds of the heart and restore multiple lives that have seemed beyond repair. You need not be a product of your past because Jesus makes all things new!

The Heavenly Father doesn't only heal our broken hearts, but He also fills them to overflowing with His love. You may have started life with a damaged heart like I did, or worse, but that doesn't determine your future! No matter what has happened to you, nothing is impossible for the Heavenly Father to heal or restore. God doesn't erase the bad memories, but He does take the pain out of them, removing their sting from your life.

God provides a way for those of us who've had less than perfect earthly fathers to receive everything we need from Him. All is not lost. We don't have to be part of another sad statistic. Even though we can't go back in time and have our earthly fathers treat us better, we *can* be restored through the loving touch of our Heavenly Father. We can still turn to Him to teach and guide us into our destiny through His perfect love.

We all want a loving father we can see, touch, and talk to face-to-face, one who will pick us up when we fall down, and tell us everything will be okay. We want him to admire us and be at our side where we

> *Even though we can't go back in time and have our earthly fathers treat us better, we can be restored through the loving touch of our Heavenly Father.*

can see him along the road of life. However, God doesn't always work that way. He is for the most part an invisible God and Father.

I believe He wants to know your heart, to know if you will seek Him by exercising your faith. This requires a childlike trust to know that He is right there with you, and the faith to believe that you will find Him. If God were visible on the earth today and could be seen by everyone, people would have no choice but to worship Him. His very presence would demand it! However, although He may not provide a physical presence at your side, He still allows those who seek Him with all their hearts to find him.

CONCLUSION

We often have a specific idea of how we want God to heal our hearts. Healing requires an unconditional surrender to Him in which we allow Him to touch us, speak to us, and heal us *His* way. He might do it through a radical God-encounter. However, Father God most often speaks to us via His still small voice, spontaneous thoughts, or daydream-like visions, which we might dismiss as insignificant or of our own imagination.

Being more attentive to how He speaks to you will help your heart become healed. He *will* speak to you, touching you in the deepest parts of your soul and healing your broken heart, if you allow Him to. He did it for me when I sought His healing for my father wound, and He will do the same for you!

ACTION CHALLENGE

1. Take a moment to examine your heart. Make a list of all of the empty spaces that a loving father should have filled.
2. Now hand these empty spaces and all of the resulting pain and longing over to God the Father. In a symbolic act, hold your hands out to Him and place all of that pain and loss into them. Ask Him to take away the pain and fill the empty spaces with His love. Ask Him to be the One Who fills you with everything you ever needed from your earthly father.
3. Allow me to pray over you: *Heavenly Father, I ask You to reveal areas that the reader needs to give over to You. Accompany them into the scary places in their heart and encounter them just as they are. Please take the negative or oppressive things away from them and give them Your liquid love and truth, in Jesus' mighty and all-powerful name.*
4. Journal your thoughts about this chapter and how God is healing the father wound in your heart.

Chapter Ten

THE ADOPTION

"And hope does not put us to shame, because God's love has been poured out into our hearts through the Holy Spirit, who has been given to us" (NIV, Romans 5:5).

There are many types of fathers in the world. Anybody who has ever lived has grown up in a home where their father is either passive, perfectionist, authoritarian, abusive, absent, a good father, or a combination of these types. Nobody is perfect, and no father is perfect either. As you evaluate the role and effect your father has had on your life, you will be able to identify negative patterns and forgive your father from your heart, receiving inner healing and an outpouring of God's supernatural liquid love in return.

NOBODY'S PERFECT

Let's begin by looking at each father type and the particular impact left on his children. It's easy to have misconceptions about Father God, because we tend to perceive Him through the same lens as we see our earthly fathers. For example, if I had a perfectionist father, I could try to please God through exemplary service in the church, or believe my worth comes from being a very disciplined and active Christian instead of a loved and valued child of God.

Depending on which case study you read, you'll find a number of different categories for the way a father is perceived by his children. I've chosen six general categories, but these are not exhaustive or diverse enough to cover everyone's experience. Nonetheless, they do serve as a good basis to describe our own experiences with our earthly fathers. We will look at each one, examining how a child feels growing up in that environment and the way it affects how he or she perceives Father God. As we do this, I invite you to identify which ones best describe your earthly father.

After speaking at a conference about these negative father types and the solution of the Heavenly Father's love, a man approached me in tears saying he embodied all the negative types in one. He repented and received a dramatic healing touch from God, and then immediately left for his teenage daughter's high school to ask her forgiveness in person. His life and his family will be forever changed!

It may be scary or painful to look at your past and present under this type of microscope, but the rewards make the effort worthwhile! As you examine yourself as a child or father, I believe God will begin to speak to you and break down the barriers that have kept you from wholeness. Let's begin!

THE ABSENT FATHER

The absent father is simply not present for his children. He might have died or abandoned the family. He could be in prison or working in another country. The absent father might be steeped in drug addiction and living on the streets or sleeping in the home but negligent of his responsibilities. There are many reasons a father might be absent, but in the end, he cannot provide what is required for his children to grow up emotionally healthy and affirmed.

HOW THE CHILD OF AN ABSENT FATHER FEELS

It is normal for the child of an absent father to feel abandoned, rejected, and left to fend for himself. There is often deep resentment. The child feels unloved and unvalued. He is insecure of himself and presents behavioral problems such as aggression, shyness, and emotional dependence. It is difficult for him to develop close and intimate relationships, since he is fearful that others will leave him as his father has done. He lives with a persistent feeling of emptiness.

HOW THE CHILD PERCEIVES GOD

He believes God will behave the same as his earthly father, so he distances himself from God. He views God as someone who created the world and then abandoned it. The child of an absent father believes God doesn't want to be involved in any aspects of his everyday life. He may feel resentment against God for not showing Himself in obvious ways, or for allowing his earthly father to desert him. The child feels abandoned by God and doesn't develop an intimate relationship with Him since he believes God does not care about him. This child rarely believes that the promises of God are his.

THE PASSIVE FATHER

The passive father is present in the home but not involved in the lives of his children. This father does not take an active part in the upbringing of his children, often making excuses for why he can't or won't spend time with them. He will often delegate or "push off" his children to his wife or other family members. He is a permissive parent who sets no limits or rules, but also doesn't rescue or help the child when help is needed.

HOW THE CHILD OF A PASSIVE FATHER FEELS

The child of a passive father feels that everyone should give her what she wants, and she finds it difficult to be obedient or respect authority figures. She is emotionally immature and tends to be impulsive. Afraid of being unprotected, she believes she must fend for herself in life. This child may have trouble making deep friendships because she feels other people don't care about her heart.

HOW THE CHILD PERCEIVES GOD

This child sees God as Someone who should give her everything and yet ask for nothing in return. It is difficult for her to walk in obedience and submit to God or spiritual leaders. Since she is used to doing as she pleases, she finds it difficult to work as a member of a team or have her character formed by a spiritual leader. She may also feel that God is distant and unconcerned about her heart.

THE PERFECTIONIST FATHER

The perfectionist father demands that his children be perfect in everything. No effort or achievement is "good enough" or satisfies the father, who is always expecting more from the child. The children of perfectionist parents are often quite frustrated with their lives. The perfectionist father requires everyone in the household to do as he says, and his rule is law. Honest mistakes are not tolerated. Religious fathers can fall into this negative pattern, thinking they are pleasing God by making their children "perfect," not understanding they are just controlling their child's behavior without addressing the heart.

HOW THE CHILD OF A PERFECTIONIST FATHER FEELS

The child of a perfectionist father feels like he's always walking on eggshells, fearing his father's disappointment. Deep down, he believes that no matter how hard he tries, he will never "measure up." Believing he must always attain high performance and achievements, he may become a perfectionist and high achiever, but for the wrong reasons. In the end, he will achieve in order to find acceptance and feel loved.

While some children of perfectionist fathers become high achievers, the opposite can also be true. A child's perfectionist upbringing might prevent him from achieving many things because he believes it's safer not to do anything at all than try his hardest and still not be good enough. He is defensive when receiving criticism and often develops anxiety and compulsive behaviors. These may cause addictions that mask the pain and frustration of striving to be perfect but never succeeding. This child feels a lot of internal anger and lies to cover up anything negative about himself for fear of disappointing others.

HOW THE CHILD PERCEIVES GOD

The child of a perfectionist father sees God as demanding and believes that nothing he can do will ever please Him. He doesn't feel loved or accepted by God and believes that he can only be loved for what he achieves for God. He sees God as a religion rather than as a relationship and believes he must first get free of his addictions or chains of slavery before he can get close to the Father and be accepted by Him.

This child doesn't understand that there is no way out of the addiction without God's help, and that he doesn't have the power to set himself free. He has trouble believing that Father God will accept him right where he is, and that he needs a relationship with Father God in order to be set free from his addiction and pain.

THE AUTHORITARIAN FATHER

The authoritarian father is like a dictator who demands unquestioned obedience. He is harsh and stern, seeing everything as black or white, right or wrong. This father is controlling and swings his power around for all to see. He is often emotionally abusive and not interested in the needs of his children. Many authoritarian fathers mistakenly feel that it is their godly right to act this way, and their children's godly duty to submit to their father.

HOW THE CHILD OF AN AUTHORITARIAN FATHER FEELS

The child of an authoritarian father feels obligated to be submissive and obey everything imposed on her, which later leads to rebellion and resentment. She is fearful of the wrath of her father and feels a deep insecurity and inner anger due to not feeling loved or valued. Many times, these children end up believing there is something inherently wrong with them, and that they deserve everything bad that happens to them. They are socially uncomfortable and introverted, preferring to take the easier road of uninvolvement rather than risk being wrong and singled out.

HOW THE CHILD PERCEIVES GOD

She believes God is angry and will punish her for not doing what He wants. She sees God as Someone who simply imposes rules on people and obliges them to serve Him. This separates her from the true love of God, and she finds it nearly impossible to see His goodness. When she receives God in her heart, she doesn't see herself as an adopted and cherished child of God, but instead as a slave or a servant who must fall in line, obeying God and working to please Him.

THE ABUSIVE FATHER

The abusive father typically causes the most damage to his children. This type of father assaults his children verbally, emotionally, physically, and/or sexually. He maintains an attitude of criticism, contempt, rejection, and constant humiliation toward them, and often treats his children more like objects than humans.

HOW THE CHILD OF AN ABUSIVE FATHER FEELS

The child of an abusive father is insecure, has low self-esteem, and tends toward depression and other mental disorders caused by trauma. She often feels a high degree of shame and constant guilt, believing she somehow had a part in the abuse. She is often emotionally repressed and has difficulty socializing. This child also lives in a constant state of fear of further abuse.

HOW THE CHILD PERCEIVES GOD

The abused child sees God as a distant father who is not interested in her. She blames God for having allowed the abuse and everything bad that has happened to her and finds it difficult to accept her own identity as a child of God. She typically has great difficulty in trusting authority figures.

THE GOOD FATHER

This is my favorite type of father. The good father is embodied in our Heavenly Father Who has the power to restore the damage caused by all the negative father types in the hearts and lives of their children. While the other father types are based on fear and control, this is the only father type based on love and relationship.

The good father is gentle and disciplines his children with love, setting appropriate guidelines and rules. He respects his children and expects them to follow through with what he asks of them. He listens to them, gives loving correction, strives to teach them, and at all times reaffirms their identity as beloved children.

The good father is both physically and emotionally present for his children and always fosters healthy connections with them. He takes time to listen and help, gives them responsibilities, and allows his children to make mistakes and learn from them. A good father values the time he spends with his children and loves to make them laugh.

> *The good father is embodied in our Heavenly Father Who has the power to restore the damage caused by all the negative father types in the hearts and lives of their children.*

HOW THE CHILD OF A GOOD FATHER FEELS

The child of a good father feels loved. He is secure, happy, and independent. He respects others, is teachable, and submits easily to authority figures. Connecting well with others comes naturally for him, and he is able to overcome problems and obstacles because he has abundant hope.

HOW THE CHILD PERCEIVES GOD

The child of a good father easily accepts God as a loving Father, and therefore finds it natural to develop a close and intimate relationship with Him. He has a positive, trusting outlook on God, seeing Him as a provider, protector, and nurturer as well as an authority figure Who deserves respect and honor. Because of this child's great trust in God, he will easily submit to God's authority and direction.

Even if this child doesn't fully understand God's direction, he gains satisfaction by being obedient to Him. He is filled with brilliant, expectant hope in every situation. His perspective of God reduces his own anxiety and stress, promotes inner peace, and creates an environment for the supernatural move of God in his life.

HOW TO RECEIVE THE FATHER'S LOVE

The most important key to receiving a supernatural impartation of the Father's healing love is to forgive your earthly father from your heart. It's not enough to simply think, *I forgive my dad for all the destructive things he did.* This won't accomplish much. The most effective way to forgive someone is by speaking it aloud and very specifically.

Something powerful happens when your own ears can hear you forgiving, even if the person you're forgiving is nowhere near. Forgiving them for specific words, actions, or situations connects your emotions (your heart) to the act and words of forgiving. It makes the forgiveness more real.

For example, I might say out loud, "In Jesus name, I forgive my dad for not playing catch that Saturday when I was ten years old. I forgive him for saying that he didn't want to play with me. This broke my heart and caused me years of pain, sadness, and loneliness. I forgive him for the hurt and brokenness it caused." Being specific will help you release the person you are forgiving from your judgement and condemnation. Let's forgive our fathers for failing us and letting us down. Let's also ask God to forgive us for the ways we have misunderstood or judged them.

WHAT IS A FATHER?

An excellent analogy to how we can receive our Heavenly Father's love can be seen through the process our adopted daughter Mariana went through as her wounds were healed. One of the first things we noticed about Mariana when she arrived at our home was that she literally had *no idea* what a father was or how to react to one. She'd been in multiple foster homes run almost entirely by single women. She didn't know how to treat me, her new father, and for the first few weeks acted a bit standoffish toward me.

One day while Mariana and Abby were having a conversation, Abby started talking about how she would like to get married someday. Mariana asked in surprise and almost disgust, "Why would you *ever* want to get *married*?"

Abby responded with humor, "So I can have a husband." Bewildered, Mariana asked why Abby would need a husband. "So I can have children," Abby replied, laughing. Mariana wondered out loud why anybody would need a husband to have children. Abby answered, "So he can be the father of my children and help take care of them."

"Why do you need a father to have children and take care of them?" Mariana insisted in all seriousness. Mariana had never known the purpose or role of a father. Based on her previous experiences, the mother could take on the roles of both the father and the mother.

In Colombia, unwed single mothers are the norm. There's a phrase here that says, "There is only one mother for me, but the father could be anybody." This shocking saying expresses the troubling absence of fatherhood in the culture, with the result that the few fathers around are considered almost second-class to the mothers. This has created a matriarchal family structure, most times out of necessity. That is the only family structure Mariana knew, so she would have to relearn what a family was by experience.

I WILL ALWAYS LOVE YOU

Every night before bed I would go to Mariana's room, look her in the eyes, and tell her how much I love her. I would say, "Mariana, I am your father and I love you so much. My love for you is unconditional. It doesn't matter if you're good or bad. I will always love you. You don't have to do anything to earn my love, and there's nothing you can do to take it away either. I will always be there for you, and I will always protect and help you. My love for you will never go away. You are my daughter."

Our Heavenly Father is saying the same things over us right now. Maybe you feel far away from God, like He's not as accessible as before, or maybe you've never had a close relationship with Him. In either case, your Heavenly Father has not left you. He is always right at your side waiting patiently for you. He will never leave you or forsake you.

BREAKTHROUGH

Mariana and I were cleaning the kitchen one afternoon while everyone else was out of the house. She was wiping down the table as I was doing the dishes when suddenly she said in a nonchalant way, "Daddy, you're a *really* good daddy!" This was an incredible breakthrough! She was understanding what a father is and does.

Just a few days later we heard some troubling news about a single-parent family in which the son and daughter were close friends of ours. They had experienced tragic domestic violence and now found themselves on the street with no money, no friends, and no place to go. We already had six people living in an average-sized house, and it would be a bit tight for all three of them to move in with us, but we certainly couldn't leave them on the street, even for a few hours!

While Jen was praying about how to best respond to their needs, God told her to look up Luke 3:11. She did, and to her astonishment it read, "Anyone who has two shirts should share with the one who has none, and anyone who has food should do the same" (*NIV*, Luke 3:11). That was all the encouragement we needed. We invited this family into our home, and they lived with us for a few months until we could get them settled into their own apartment.

LIKE A FATHER

The daughter of the family was a little younger than Mariana and had not benefited from the presence of a healthy and involved father in her life. At this point, neither of the girls knew how to ride a bike, so over a few weeks' time I taught them both how to ride. The friend didn't know how to swim either, and since we have a pool, this was another life skill I knew she must learn as quickly as possible. I started giving her swimming classes, and within a few weeks she was able to swim independently in the pool.

We all ate together every night, and during one of these dinners Mariana pointed at her friend and blurted out, as if she'd just had an amazing revelation, "Daddy, you're her daddy too! You're teaching her to ride a bike like you're teaching me, you're taking care of her like you're taking care of me, and you're encouraging her like you encourage me. She doesn't have her real daddy, so you're her daddy!" Wow, she'd finally gotten it!

In the same way, the Heavenly Father will show you if you let him. Mariana's revelation can be your revelation. Earthly adoption is something we know and can relate to, and it's an excellent starting point to understand our Heavenly adoption. It never occurred to me how much God would teach me about *His* adoption of *me* through *our* adoption of *Mariana*. Being obedient to His leading in this area brought amazing blessings to me and my family and has shed light on the Father heart of God.

CONCLUSION

No matter which negative father influences you have had in your life, it is never too late to receive the influence of the Good Father. His influence in your life will gradually replace and erase the negative influences you have been subjected to during your stay on the earth. The bad things that have happened to you were not brought on by Him, nor were they part of His plan for your life. They were a result of sin and corruption in the world, and the plans of the devil.

God can take what was meant for evil and harm and turn it around for your good and the good of others. Just take the first step of trying to see Him as the Good Father and begin to trust Him. The following verse can bring transformation to your life right now. Jesus is talking to the Heavenly Father not only about His disciples but about all of His children when He says, "I have made you known to them, and will continue to make you known in order that the love you have for me may be in them and that I myself may be in them" (*NIV*, John 17:26).

Jesus uttered this prayer just a few days before He died, and in it He promised to continue revealing the Father to the disciples after He left the earth. He is praying for an impartation of the Father's Love when He says, "that the love you have for me may be in them." Therefore, whenever Jesus reveals to you aspects of the Heavenly Father, an impartation of the Father's Love is also included!

ACTION CHALLENGE

1. Take a moment and forgive your earthly father just as we explained in this chapter. Ask the Holy Spirit to reveal to you all the things you need to forgive, then do it out loud and specifically. It may help to write them down in a list. As you feel the negative emotions rise, give them to Jesus. Afterwards, ask Jesus what He gives you in place of all those negative thoughts and feelings.

2. Now, ask the Holy Spirit for a fresh impartation of the Father's love. Close your eyes and open your hands, holding them out in a gesture to God that shows you are ready to receive from Him.

3. Allow me to pray over you: *Heavenly Father, I pray that everyone reading these words would receive an impartation of Your divine, tangible love right now, in Jesus' name. I ask You to fill each one to overflowing with Your liquid love.*

4. Journal your thoughts about this chapter and how God is healing the father wound in your heart.

Chapter Eleven

ARE YOU ADOPTED?

*"But as many as received Him, to them He gave
the right to become children of God, to those who
believe in His name" (NKJV, John 1:12).*

Did you ever think about the fact that nobody is *forced* to adopt? Parents adopt because they choose to. It comes from an overflow of love in their hearts which compels them to be decisive and assertive until they accomplish their goal. Adoption is not a passive thing. Adoptive parents often have to exert an exceptional amount of time, energy, perseverance, tenacity, and finances to adopt. Sometimes it takes several years, large sums of money, and even fighting against obstacles that get in the way, before an adoption goes through.

What makes a person become willing to sacrifice and fight so much to contend for someone they do not even know and with whom they have no biological connection? The only plausible answer is that God places His love in people, even those who do not know or recognize Him, causing them to seek out and rescue the lost. This love is a pure grace and gift for humanity, pointing back to the extravagant love of the Heavenly Father.

When a person receives Jesus as their Savior and becomes His disciple, they also experience adoption - adoption by the Heavenly Father!

However, this adoption required an outrageous price and an exorbitant sacrifice, which Jesus paid by choosing to live on Earth and give His life for every son and daughter who would accept Him. There is no higher price one could pay, no higher value a parent could place on an adopted child's life, than to give their own life as payment for the adoption!

CHOSEN

While living in Colombia we discovered that adoption is free for residents and citizens. Many of our friends in the United States have adopted, and we knew it could be very difficult for the family. Although content with our three delightful biological children, Jen felt a powerful desire to pursue the adoption of a fourth child. I, on the other hand, was more hesitant. After all, things were going well for our family. In addition, the ministry took up so much time and energy that I wondered if it would be wise to disrupt our lives with what could be a difficult adoption.

There is no higher price one could pay, no higher value a parent could place on an adopted child's life, than to give their own life as payment for the adoption!

Pausing after prayer, I sensed God reminding me of the great peace and love He had placed in our family, and the grace He had given my wife and me to overcome many obstacles in both of our backgrounds. He said, "Open your arms a little wider and allow someone else to experience this grace and blessing, too. After all, I'm the One Who has given you this gift of a healthy family."

The thought crossed my mind that someday while lying on my deathbed I wouldn't want to have the nagging question and regret in my mind, *what would have happened if we'd tried to adopt?* I knew we felt called to adopt and were able to do so, thus I had no excuse to avoid taking the first step of the process.

A quote from Mother Teresa came to mind, which says, "The problem with the world is that we draw the circle of our family too small." The Father, Son, and Holy Spirit are like a family, and yet God drew an enormous circle around the Trinity to include everyone who would ever accept Him. He chose to adopt us, just as we would choose to adopt our Colombian daughter.

OUT THERE SOMEWHERE

With Jen, the kids, and now me on board, we had the crazy faith that out there in adoption-land was a girl under ten years of age who could control her emotions, who wouldn't bring too much chaos into our family, and who just needed a loving and nurturing environment in which to flourish.

We recognized that this was somewhat unrealistic, rather like a fairytale thought. Having worked for years with at-risk and vulnerable populations in the city, I was very familiar with the biological families, neighborhoods, and atrocities these kids have to endure before their placement in adoptive families.

In addition, I was aware of the many kinds of abuse and dreadful situations that happen to many of the kids in the system. It would either be delusion or divine intervention mixed with blind faith in a loving God that would keep us believing that a special, healthy, older girl was out there waiting for us. We reasoned that since we were confident God was calling us to adopt, He wouldn't give us more than we could handle. Knowing this, we proceeded with the adoption process, praying daily that God would guide each step.

THE CALL

Four years after filling out all the paperwork, taking adoption classes, fulfilling psychological evaluations and home visits, and sending in reports on our family, the phone rang, and a case worker shared that the adoption committee had chosen a nine-year-old girl for our family!

From reading the file we could see that although Mariana had gone from foster home to foster home for most of her short life, she was resilient, outgoing, and able to form connections with people. I knew that no matter what she had been through, if she could form a connection with us, divine healing would flow through that connection to heal her heart, emotions, and soul. Our answer was a resounding, "Yes"!

ADOPTION IS IRREVOCABLE

Shortly after the judge approved the adoption and Mariana came home, I met with our lawyer at the courthouse to receive and process the adoption papers. As I began to read the official sentencing documents, the presence of the Lord came over me. I sensed God whispering to me, "Pay attention to what you are reading, because this is the same process in which I adopted and accepted you into My family."

The legal document established in clear language: *This adoption is irrevocable. There is no legal way to undo this adoption. It is final and forever. Even if the parents decide they do not want the child anymore, they cannot un-adopt the child.* In like manner, God the Father's adoption of us is permanent and can never be undone. That's how strong His love is for us. When He "signs" for your adoption, it's permanent!

FIVE GIFTS OF AN ADOPTED CHILD

Through the adoption process I began to live and experience the Father's heart for what it means for us to be adopted into God's family.

This spiritual adoption is available for everyone who accepts and receives Jesus as their Savior and Lord. There are five specific things an adopted child receives, and if you pay attention, you'll see that we receive those same five things when we are adopted by the Heavenly Father!

1. A NEW IDENTITY

From reading Mariana's file, I learned about her biological family and the neighborhood in which they lived. I thought there might be potential problems if they found out Mariana's adoptive family were Americans living within twenty minutes of their run-down neighborhood. Being familiar with slum neighborhoods, it also concerned me that if they started looking for her, they could find us and cause harm through extortion and threats. However, when I asked our lawyer if there was any way the family could find her by looking in the databases, he said this would be impossible because as an adopted child she receives a brand-new identity!

The lawyer's response taught me something very important not just about adoption, but also about the Kingdom of Heaven. Identity changes are *retroactive*, meaning our adopted child receives a new birth certificate. A birth certificate always identifies three people: the child, the father, and the mother. In Mariana's case, she received a new birth certificate with our names appearing as her father and mother. If someone were to go to the official birth records office and request Mariana's birth certificate to figure out whose child she is, they would discover that she is a daughter of Thomas and Jennifer Atwater.

The same thing happens when God adopts us into His family. The Bible describes this in 2 Corinthians, which says, "Therefore, if anyone is in Christ, the new creation has come: The old has gone, the new is here" (*NIV*, 2 Corinthians 5:17)! A new creation speaks about a new identity, and a new identity speaks about a new destiny and purpose for the person. Mariana's life will forever be marked by the times before and after adoption, because the adoption changed everything about her life. Being adopted into a new family meant that there were new opportunities, new experiences, and a new world to explore.

2. A NEW NAME

As soon as the adoption was official, Mariana's former last name changed and she received a new last name - Atwater - which will forever be part of her identity. This is documented on a new birth certificate which shows our name, representing her new family line. Her first name stays the same, meaning she is still "herself." She doesn't lose the essence of who she is or her personality.

The same thing happens to those who are adopted by Father God. Our new name becomes "Child of God!" John 1:12 says, "Yet to all who did receive him, to those who believed in his name, he gave the right to become children of God" (*NIV*, John 1:12). Likewise, in the book of Revelation it says, "I will also give that person a white stone with a new name written on it" (*NIV*, Revelation 2:17b). Like Mariana, when Father God adopts us, we don't lose our essence or our personality. We remain ourselves yet become filled with God and His Spirit. We take on His family name - "Child of God!"

3. A NEW INHERITANCE

The sentencing documents continued to explain that our adopted daughter has a legal right to the inheritance of our family. Part of the adoption commitment is to include your adopted child in your inheritance. This is set in stone and cannot be changed. Likewise, we must realize that our adoption into God's family includes a very large inheritance!

The following verses mention this amazing inheritance:

- "...and giving joyful thanks to the Father, who has qualified you to share in the *inheritance* [emphasis added] of his holy people in the kingdom of light" (*NIV*, Colossians 1:12).
- "If you belong to Christ, then you are Abraham's seed, and *heirs* [emphasis added] according to the promise" (*NIV*, Galatians 3:29).
- "Now if we are children, then we are *heirs*—*heirs* [emphasis added] of God and *co-heirs* [emphasis added] with Christ, if indeed we share in his sufferings in order that we may also share in his glory" (*NIV*, Romans 8:17).

As adopted children of God, we have a right to His inheritance. What is an inheritance? It's your birthright, what you receive from the people who gave you birth when they die. Jesus has given us spiritual birth into the family of God. When He died, this Heavenly inheritance was released to His children, the rightful and legal heirs of the promises of God. This inheritance cannot be denied or revoked.

Our spiritual inheritance includes the following and much, much more:

- The very power that raised Jesus from the dead (Romans 8:11)
- The promise of the infilling of the Holy Spirit (Luke 24:49)
- Forgiveness of our sins (1 John 1:9)
- Eternal life with Him (John 3:16)
- Divine physical healing (Psalm 103:2-3)
- Freedom from oppression (1 John 5:4-5)
- Peace (John 14:27)
- An abundant life filled with love and compassion (John 10:10b)
- Renewed strength (Isaiah 40:31)
- Financial miracles (Proverbs 10:22)
- Favor (Psalm 5:12)
- Being seated with Jesus in Heavenly places (Ephesians 2:6)
- Deep communion and union with God (Galatians 2:20)

What an incredible inheritance! I know it sounds too good to be true, but it's not! Don't let the lies of the enemy deceive you. As sons and daughters of the living God, we must rise and take our rightful positions as His children. We must declare these truths over ourselves and start walking them out in our everyday lives!

4. A NEW CITIZENSHIP

The analogy between earthly adoption and Heavenly adoption is even more exaggerated in our case. We are citizens of the United States of America, sent on a mission to an unfamiliar country, Colombia, in which we adopted Mariana. Because of the adoption, Mariana is now a citizen of a new country (kingdom). She has full access to all the rights and privileges of the new "kingdom." There are countless new opportunities available to her as a citizen of the United States of America, and she has full access to all of them!

The same is true for the adopted children of Father God. They become citizens of a new Kingdom and receive all the rights and privileges that come with being members of that Heavenly Kingdom. This is true for you and me. When we are adopted into the Kingdom of God, we become citizens of Heaven!

Paul mentions this when he says, "But our citizenship is in Heaven. And we eagerly await a Savior from there, the Lord Jesus Christ" (*NIV*, Philippians 3:20). He later adds, "For he has rescued us from the dominion of darkness and brought us into the kingdom of the Son he loves" (*NIV*, Colossians 1:13). What a great inheritance awaits us!

5. A NEW CULTURE

Mariana's adjustment to our family was smooth considering the great difficulty many adopted children have. Even so, there was a definite adaptation process that even now we experience from time to time. Our daughter Abby is just seventeen months older than Mariana. Although Abby treated her new sister with kindness and respect, for the first few months after the adoption, Mariana would do cruel things to Abby, such as ripping up her artwork, breaking something special of hers on purpose, or just being unkind toward her.

We had loving yet firm conversations with Mariana explaining that she is now part of a new family with a new culture. We don't operate the same as the foster families with whom she lived. The basis of our culture is love, honor, and respect, and we will fight to protect that culture. This meant that if Mariana wasn't loving, honoring, or respectful toward Abby, we would protect Abby and our family culture. However, the opposite was also true. If anyone was not loving, honoring, or respectful to Mariana, we would protect her as well.

Mariana needed to change the way she thought, because what had worked in her previous culture no longer worked in this new one. She had to think of both herself and others through a different lens and with greater respect. Much of this new culture was the opposite of what she had learned and experienced in her earlier life in foster homes. It is the same adjustment we experience while becoming accustomed to the new culture of Heaven. You see, when we enter the Kingdom of God as new believers, we must change the way we think.

Many things appear to be upside down in God's Kingdom. For example, Jesus teaches that if you want to be a leader, you must be a servant. In addition, in the Heavenly economy you receive only when you give, whereas in the worldly kingdom you need to take in order to receive. Those who are first in the worldly kingdom will be last in the Heavenly Kingdom, while in the worldly kingdom those who are last often go unnoticed and unappreciated. In the worldly kingdom one must earn the love of others, yet in the Heavenly Kingdom we receive love through grace and mercy, not on the basis of merit.

Old habits die hard, and so often we want to use worldly strategies to get ahead in the Heavenly Kingdom. We think with a slave and poverty mentality instead of thinking as sons and daughters of the Most High King.

CONCLUSION

The only reason Mariana wouldn't be able to access her new identity, name, citizenship, culture, and inheritance, is if she were to believe a lie. For example, let's imagine her biological family could find and talk to her. Let's imagine their intentions were evil, and they wanted to take advantage of her and us. They could tell her that this adoption thing is just a scam, that it's too good to be true, and that she has no true citizenship or right to the United States.

They could try to make her believe that the inheritance is a lie, too. By believing these lies, she would be robbed of incredible blessings. While in reality she would have every right to go to the United States and enjoy all of the benefits and opportunities it offers, she might never go because she would be believing the lie that these rights are not hers and that she doesn't have access to them.

Imagine if her biological family would tell her she's no good and doesn't belong in her adopted family (our kingdom). What if they told her that because of her past, she would always belong to the old life and kingdom, and that she would always be out of place in the new life and kingdom? Mariana could believe those lies, leaving all the promises and assurances of the future and going back to her old life of poverty, darkness, abuse, violence, and depression.

The *greatest threat* for an adopted child is believing a lie that would rob them of their adoption rights. The same is true for an adopted child of God. That's why the enemy's language is that of lies. It's the only way he can defraud you of your new identity, name, citizenship, culture, and inheritance in Christ Jesus!

The devil, the world, and the flesh (our old sin nature) will do everything they can to rob you of these things, trying to make you unfruitful and miserable in this new adopted life with Jesus. The law of the land forever terminated Mariana's biological family's legal rights, never again to be reinstated. In the same way, if you are an adopted son or daughter of Father God, the devil's legal rights to you are forever terminated by the law of God, never again to be reinstated!

ACTION CHALLENGE

1. Take a moment and ask the Holy Spirit to reveal any lies you have believed about your identity in Jesus or your inheritance as a child of God.

2. Write them in your journal and then forgive out loud the people who have contributed to those lies in your life, including yourself. Ask God's forgiveness for believing these lies.

3. Break the lies and cancel the agreements with demons you have unknowingly made by accepting the lie. Say, "In Jesus' name, I break the lie that _____. In Jesus' name I cancel any agreement I have made with demons based on having believed this lie."

4. Ask God to tell you the truth about your identity and write it in your journal. Say, "God, if it's a lie that _____, then what is the truth?" Then begin to declare this truth over yourself every day.

Chapter Twelve

THE EXTRAVAGANT FATHER AND THE LOST SONS

"'My son,' the father said, 'you are always with me, and everything I have is yours'" (NIV, Luke 15:31).

Jesus tells a captivating story in the Bible to illustrate the heart of the extravagant, loving, Heavenly Father. I like to call the story "The Extravagant Father" even though it's better known as "The Prodigal Son." The unrestrained way in which the father loves the younger son despite his rebellious and callous behavior, and the older son despite his anger and resentment, could be called extravagant. This is the same way in which our Heavenly Father loves us.

THE YOUNGER SON

This is a story of two sons and their wealthy father. According to custom, the sons were each entitled to their share of their father's wealth when he died. The younger of the two sons got the knuckleheaded idea to acquire his fortune early, and told his dad to hand over his share of the inheritance so he could run away and do his own thing. This son was treating his dad as if he didn't matter, in essence saying, "I wish you were dead so I could get your money. Just give me what's mine and I'll be off."

This was a huge dishonor to a father in the Jewish culture of that time. The laws decreed the death penalty for sons who disrespected their fathers. Instead of killing his son, however, the father gave him half of everything he had. This rebellious son traveled to a faraway country and squandered the money on booze, parties, and women.

This beloved son thought of himself as an orphan alone in the world with no family, although in reality he had a wonderful, caring, and wealthy family. He was searching elsewhere for significance than through his natural identity as a son. He despised his father's advice, believing that easy money was better than hard-earned money. As it turns out, this "easy money" cost him almost everything.

The money ran out as water runs through a sieve, and he had to take a job feeding pigs. This son had sunk to the level of his orphan mentality, which had now stripped him not only of his family but also of his friends, his money, and his dignity. He was starving and realized the pigs ate and lived far better than he did. With nothing left to lose, this son came to his senses and went back to his father to repent and ask forgiveness, hoping his father would hire him on as a mere servant.

WHAT DOES THE YOUNGER SON RECEIVE?

Seeing his son from far away, the father is filled with such love, joy, and emotion that he runs to meet him. Throwing his arms around his son and kissing him, the father then gives him several items which demonstrate complete forgiveness and the son's restoration into the family. He gives his son sandals, a robe, a ring, and a fattened calf.

SANDALS FOR SHAME

Being barefoot outside in those times was reserved for those who were in captivity or in extreme poverty and shame. It was also a sign of those who were mourning or in grief. When the father put sandals on him, it was to take away his son's poverty and shame. The father wanted to turn his son's mourning and grief into joy and release him from his captivity.

Many people walk around in mental captivity. Much like this son, they are prisoners to the shame of their past. Mourning their life and their choices, many even fall into depression, held captive to the thought that they will always live as an orphan.

If this is you, you need to know that the loving Father is willing and waiting to receive you. Nothing you've done is beyond His forgiveness, and He *will* take away the shame of your past mistakes. He is faithful to forgive you if you confess to Him. Allow Him to put new sandals on your bare feet!

A ROBE FOR FILTH

Robes represented status and cleanliness in Jewish culture. One would never wear a beautiful robe on top of dirty clothes or an unwashed body. The Bible says that in Heaven we will receive a white robe of righteousness. When the loving father put a robe on his son, he was declaring his son clean and righteous in his eyes. He was declaring forgiveness for his son. You may not feel clean or righteous, but if you have received Jesus and given your life to Him, the Father sees you that way. You just have to believe Him and see yourself as He sees you.

A RING FOR DISGRACE

In ancient Israel, rings were given as a sign of favor and authority, and worn by wealthy, powerful men. With a signet ring one could buy, sell, and sign documents. It was for all practical purposes a debit card to the family bank account. When the father put a ring on his son's finger, he made him a full member of the family again, complete with all the rights and privileges the son had rejected when he ran away from home.

RESTORATION OF FAVOR AND AUTHORITY

What extravagant love! What a heart of forgiveness and unconditional love! The father didn't make the son wait six months or a year to prove he was ready to be let back in. He was saying, "You're back, and you're forgiven. Take your place in this family and let's pick up where we left off!" He wastes no time in restoring his son's favor and authority.

A FATTENED CALF

Celebrating with a fattened calf in that time and culture was a significant event reserved only for special occasions. This was the last part of signing an important contract or covenant between two people, or when solidifying the reconciliation between two people or groups. It's no coincidence that the father celebrated his younger son's return with a fattened calf.

The father was celebrating for three specific reasons. First, this was a special occasion and he was elated to see his son. Second, they were celebrating the new covenant they now had as father and son. In this covenant the son became a true noble son with all the rights and privileges. Third, this celebration commemorated the reconciliation of the son through his repentance to the loving father.

THE FEAST OF ALL FEASTS

The Bible foretells of the joyous feast of all feasts when the saints in Christ will attend the supper of the Lamb. The Heavenly Father will organize this celebration to welcome home all of God's sons and daughters with rejoicing. It is also to commemorate the new covenant and reconciliation of these sons and daughters who will, after much anticipation, be home forever in the Father's house. What a splendid picture of God's plan for you and me!

You might be behaving as a rebellious son or daughter of Father God. If so, Jesus is giving you the message through this story that when you're ready to come back to the Father's house, He will embrace you with open arms.

THE OLDER SON

Did you remember that the extravagant and loving father had two sons? The older son never rebelled against his father, instead serving him in the fields year after year. However, when the older brother saw that his father had restored the younger brother, he was angry toward both of them.

Luke 15:28-30 says, "The older brother became angry and refused to go in. So his father went out and pleaded with him. But he answered his father, 'Look! All these years I've been *slaving* [emphasis added] for you and never disobeyed your orders. Yet you never gave me even a young goat so I could celebrate with my friends. But when this son of yours who has squandered your property with prostitutes comes home, you kill the fattened calf for him'" (*NIV*, Luke 15:28-30)!

This older son thought of himself more as a servant or slave than as a son. He even mentions that he was "slaving." Slaving is working hard while achieving no real benefit for oneself. A slave or servant does what they are told and tries not to get into trouble. It is typical for a slave to be afraid of the one in charge, and fear drives his work and achievements. There's no reward, just more work.

Fear drove this son because he did not understand or know the heart of his father. Why didn't the son know his own father's heart? I surmise it's because he didn't reach out to connect with and get to know his father better. He did his father's work but didn't spend time in his father's presence.

Isn't this the same reason so many people today don't know the heart of their Heavenly Father? Isn't it because they don't seek Him out or spend time alone in His presence? We get so busy doing the *work* of the Father that we forget that *He Himself* is our goal. Knowing Him better, and not just working for Him, must be our greatest ambition.

ENSLAVED BY LIES

In this story of "The Extravagant Father," why do you think the older son didn't spend time getting to know his father's heart? I suggest it's because he believed a lie. His father was very wealthy, powerful, and influential. The son may have had a misconception of his father as being distant and not interested in him. He also might have thought it's best to stay away from such a powerful person so as not to get hurt or punished.

> *We get so busy doing the work of the Father that we forget that He Himself is our goal.*

He may have thought of his father as authoritarian. This would mean that the son's lack of connection with his father resulted from having fed on lies instead of the truth. Isn't this the same reason so many people today don't seek Father God? They believe He is a powerful authoritarian figure who would rather punish us than hold us in His loving embrace. However, the father's actions proved he was merciful, gentle, and full of grace when he forgave and accepted the younger son who had humbled himself, repented, and sought out his father.

At the same time, fear, lies, and jealousy blinded the older son. A person with a slave or servant mentality does not consider themselves within the vision of a family or organization. They are just workers and don't feel ownership, because slaves own nothing. Yet a person who can accept that they are truly a son or daughter has a unique view of things. They will fight for connection and support the vision and culture of the family or organization because they know they have a place and stake in it. Jesus said, "Now a slave has no permanent place in the family, but a son belongs to it forever" (*NIV*, John 8:35).

RIGHTS AND PRIVILEGES

The ironic thing is that the older son already had all the rights and privileges. He couldn't take advantage of them, however, because he was lost in a false narrative in his mind of who he was. He had created an entire fictitious world in his head that kept him trapped in the lies he believed. On the outside he looked fine and did the right things, but on the inside he was just as lost as the younger son, because he had neglected his relationship with his father.

When we believe the devil's lies, we end up separated from a true, caring, and close relationship with our loving Heavenly Father. We were born to know and connect to Him. John 17:3 says, "Now this is eternal life: that they *know* [emphasis added] you, the only true God, and Jesus Christ, whom you have sent" (*NIV*, John 17:3).

THE FATHER'S RESPONSE

As the father heard his older son's response, he observed the hurt in his son's heart. Seeing the fear, accusations, and distorted truth, he responded with loving wisdom. The father's reply is beautiful and full of meaning.

Remember, the father gave three physical items to his younger son: the ring, the robe, and sandals. He also gave three things to the older son, but they were not tangible items. Instead, they were revelations or truths. My guess is that the older son already had sandals, a robe, and a family ring, yet something even more important was missing.

MY DEAR SON

Here is what happened. "'My son,' the father said, 'you are always with me, and everything I have is yours.'" (*NIV*, Luke 15:31). The first phrase, "My son," is a phrase of endearment, of closeness. In the New Living Translation, it is translated as, "My dear son." That phrase also means, "My beloved son." The father is expressing His deepest love for His son, but the son isn't receiving the love, either because he doesn't *know* he is loved, or he doesn't *believe* it.

Imagine someone loving you with a profound and genuine love, yet you never realize it. What a loss! We are all in desperate need of love. Now visualize the innumerous loving thoughts and actions of Father God toward you, yet you are never aware of them. Could it be that God loves you more than you ever imagined or dreamed? Could it be that He has pursued you all of your life to break through the lies in your heart? What if He did all of that so that He could embrace you with tender affection, call you His own, and love you to life, healing the hurts in the darkest places of your tattered heart?

What if the very words "my beloved son" or "my beloved daughter" could break through the hard outer layer of your heart and reach your inmost parts, allowing you to experience a love unlike anything you've ever known? By an act of faith, I encourage you to open your heart a little more and receive these words from Father God: "You are My beloved child."

YOU ARE ALWAYS WITH ME

The second thing the father reveals to the older son is, "you are always with me." This means that the son has always been in his father's presence although he did not recognize it. The son felt abandoned or left out when in reality he was right there with his father the whole time.

Many times we feel as if we're just going through the motions of serving God, but don't believe He is satisfied with us. We may try to perform or do good works so that somehow we will get noticed and be rewarded, while all the time God is by our side delighting more in us than in our work.

We shouldn't be directed by what we feel or see, but by His Word and His promises. Even though we don't always feel Him next to us or even sense His presence, God assures us He is always with us and will never leave us. The Bible says, "For we live by faith, not by sight" (NIV, 2 Corinthians 5:7). When God says He is with us, it's our

> *Even though we don't always feel Him next to us or even sense His presence, God assures us He is always with us and will never leave us.*

job to believe that He is by our side. He is working in us, touching us in the depths of our hearts, whether or not we feel it.

It is by faith that we believe and receive from the Father. By an act of faith, I invite you to enter His presence and believe He is at your side. Whether or not you feel Him, He is always with you!

EVERYTHING I HAVE IS YOURS

The third phrase the father says to his oldest son is, "everything I have is yours." This son was jealous that the younger son received a party while he never had. If we look deeper, we can understand what the father is communicating. He is saying, "Since all I have is yours, you could have thrown yourself a party anytime!" However, this son was blinded by his slave mentality and couldn't believe he just needed to reach his hand out to take and use that which had been available the whole time.

CONCLUSION

You may be like the younger son in this story, afraid to go back and face your Heavenly Father because you fear you've strayed too far. Perhaps you are more like the older son, believing things that aren't true about your Heavenly Father and living your life based on some of the same lies. Maybe you haven't fallen into drugs and prostitution, but where do you go for refuge in times of difficulty or pain? Do you trust your Heavenly Father enough to go to Him? Do you trust that He will meet your needs, calm your hurting heart, and soothe your anxiety?

I invite you to quiet your mind, examine your life, and think about what needs to change. Are there false perceptions or lies you're believing about God that you need to talk over with Him? When you realize how much your Heavenly Father loves you, your life will change in dramatic ways for the better!

ACTION CHALLENGE

1. Do you have any attitudes or thoughts that reflect an orphan or slave mentality? Take a moment and ask God to forgive you for this.
2. Imagine that this very moment you are receiving from your Heavenly Father sandals, a robe, and a ring, along with their prophetic significance. Take a moment to let the truth of your Heavenly inheritance and relationship with the Father settle into your spirit.
3. Imagine yourself receiving from Father God the words, "My beloved child, you have always been at my side and everything I have is yours." Take time to let those words sink deep into your soul.
4. Write your thoughts in a journal.

Chapter Thirteen

THE WITCH, THE SHAMAN, AND THE LIGHT

"...to open their eyes and turn them from darkness to light, and from the power of Satan to God, so that they may receive forgiveness of sins and a place among those who are sanctified by faith in me" (NIV, Acts 26:18).

I magine you are in a pitch-black room with the lights turned off. The doors and window shades are shut tight, not letting in any light from the midday sun. This room is so dark it's impossible to see your way around. Now imagine opening the window shade and allowing the outside light to pour into the room. At once, everything is visible and all the darkness is gone.

This is what happens when the light of Jesus enters the darkness in our lives. The darkness doesn't need to be conquered and overcome as much as the light needs to be let in. Once the light is let in, the darkness vanishes, often without a fight.

It's encouraging to see the love and power of God at work in tangible ways. The following stories demonstrate how the Lord is always protecting and loving His children in marvelous ways. We hope they inspire you to believe the promises of God in the Bible for those who follow Him with all their hearts. He is always there to love, help, and protect His children. Every time we think there is no way out, He surprises us with uncanny creativity and divine intervention. Our job is simple - we are to trust and obey Him.

THE WITCH AND HER FOUR-YEAR-OLD DAUGHTER

"We have a gigantic problem!" our teacher coordinator exclaimed as she rushed with eyes wide open into my office. A few days before, we had received a new four-year-old student in one of the preschool classrooms at the children's center we directed. Her teacher had reported that the little girl manifested demons every time worship music was played during their daily prayer and worship time. The child's face would contort, her body would tense up, and she would begin to shake, crying and screaming in an angry voice, "*Turn it off! Turn it off!*"

This small child wore a ritual amulet necklace which people in the occult wear for "protection" against evil spirits, hoping it will counter any spells put against them. The irony is that these amulets and rituals seem to attract more evil spirits than they repel, although those living in darkness cannot see that.

The coordinator had been in the classroom and had witnessed with her own eyes what this child went through during worship and prayer time. Now she was asking permission to deliver the girl from demonic oppression in the name of Jesus. Receiving a prodding from the Holy Spirit, I surprised both of us by saying, "No, we are not going to deliver the child." Although I had no idea who the child's mother was, I sensed and declared, "Her mother is going to deliver her and set her free, because her mother is somehow involved with this situation and has authority over her child."

I instructed the teacher to remove the little girl from the class during worship times until she received freedom. There were two reasons for this. First, the demons were torturing her during worship, and we did not want her to suffer more. Second, the tantrum they put on distracted the rest of the class from worshiping Jesus. These demons were taking the attention off the King of kings and putting it on themselves.

DEMONIZED

We discussed how to best approach the child's mother. It could be a bit strange to approach a woman you've never met and tell her that her preschool daughter is demonized. It's funny how we always seem to find ourselves in challenging new situations for which we don't yet have the necessary wisdom. This drives us to the feet and mercy of Jesus and promotes a lifestyle of complete dependence on God. We are so fortunate to be living in a place where we cannot fulfill our job or destiny without God's explicit help. We must depend on His wisdom and love in every moment!

The strategy I sensed from God was for the coordinator not to mention the word 'demon' to the mother, but to describe in plain language what was happening during worship. We would see where the conversation went and watch for the mother's reaction. I urged the coordinator to pray and be guided by the Holy Spirit.

A few days later she rushed into my office again, blurting out with urgency, "I talked to the child's mother and we have a *much bigger* problem! The mother has been practicing witchcraft since she was a little girl. We are dealing with a witch!" Although this was a Christ-centered organization, we allowed anyone from the community into our programs. Our clients understand that we operated from a Biblical point of view, but that we wouldn't force our views on them.

The coordinator explained how the previous month the mother and daughter had moved to Medellín from the Chocó region of Colombia, an area well-known for its witchcraft. The mother believed she and her daughter were being attacked by evil spirits another witch had sent to oppress them. Her entire family was suffering from many strange infirmities. In response, the mother created a "protection" charm to put around her daughter's neck.

INVISIBLE HANDS

"What do I do?" asked the coordinator.

"Well," I replied, "introduce the mom to Jesus. He's irresistible! Talk to her about His power, His authority, and His love. Show her what Jesus says about witchcraft and divination in the Bible and let her know that Jesus does not agree with what she is doing."

I continued, "Also, tell her about Jesus' protection, which is greater than any other spirit, charm, amulet, or spell anyone could ever make. Show her the amazing protection of Jesus in Psalm 91 for those who trust in Him and find their refuge in Him instead of in other things. Explain that Jesus is present in the room with you both, that He is real and trustworthy, and that if she would put her trust in Him rather than the amulet necklace, He will protect them!"

The coordinator accepted the instructions and went off to meet once again with the mother. She explained pertinent Scripture passages about the power and love of Jesus, which helped the mother to better understand the situation. The mother did not want to offend Jesus and now desired to follow His instructions for her life. She renounced her past and put her life in the hands of Jesus!

What this woman did next took supernatural faith because she had practiced witchcraft since she was a girl. This wicked power was the only power she'd ever known, and she'd trusted in it throughout her life. In a courageous step of faith, she removed the amulet necklace from her beloved daughter's neck, and then put her daughter into the invisible hands of Jesus, trusting in the promises of Psalm 91.

The very next day, the little girl's teacher forgot to exclude her during worship. As the music was playing and the other children were praising, the girl realized there was no evil manifestation inside her, and she jumped up and down in surprise and joyful gratitude. She began praising the Lord, yelling, "Look! I'm not upset! I'm not crying!" The mother had been instrumental in the deliverance of her child, which was accomplished when the love and power of Jesus overcame the darkness and displaced it with the light.

These situations are a definite reminder that our battle is not against flesh and blood, but against spiritual forces unseen by the natural eye. Paul describes this in Ephesians 6:12, where he writes, "For our struggle is not against flesh and blood, but against the rulers, against the authorities, against the powers of this dark world and against the spiritual forces of evil in the heavenly realms" (*NIV*, Ephesians 6:12).

The light of Jesus is powerful enough to not only shine in the lives of people who once were against him like this ex-witch, but also to break the hold of diseases that devastate neighborhoods and communities. The following story demonstrates how this light not only reveals the origin of diseases but can stop them in their tracks.

CHICKENPOX FROM HELL

Several preschoolers were coming down with chickenpox at the children's center. Although we'd sent them home right away to recover, the disease had still spread until five of our six classrooms each had multiple cases. This was of great concern not only for the health of these at-risk children, but also because we would soon need to alert the Health Department and they might shut down the center for up to several months. This would mean the children wouldn't receive the three daily meals they were getting with us.

I found it curious, however, that one of our six classrooms had no cases. Even more perplexing, some of the students in this class had siblings in other classrooms who *did* have chickenpox. These families don't live in houses, but in rented ten-by-ten-foot rooms in filthy, drug-ridden slum buildings with bathrooms, showers, and kitchens shared by everyone who lives on the floor. The entire family may share a single mattress and blanket. Living in this environment, it would be impossible for siblings not to catch chickenpox from each other.

Even more interesting was the fact that the teacher of this room carried more of the presence of God than any other teacher at that time. I asked her why there were no cases in her room. She said that once she heard there were cases of chickenpox in the institution, she felt God telling her to anoint the door of her classroom. She and her teaching assistant had anointed the door and prayed, declaring to the virus, "You will pass no further in Jesus' name." They prayed over the room and over each child. The results were nothing less than miraculous. The virus touched no child in her room - a supernatural protection!

Sensing that this was not a simple virus outbreak but something more spiritual, I sent both that teacher and our coordinator, who also carried the presence of God, to the room where the chickenpox started. I wanted them to kick that virus and everything with it out of the children's center! Here the story gets almost unbelievable. As soon as they both stepped over the threshold of the door of the classroom, chickenpox started to appear on each of their faces!

Although this took them both by surprise, the coordinator shook off her fear and said, "The devil is a liar, and these are his tricks." She told the teacher, "I will pray for you and then you pray for me." As she prayed in Jesus' name, within seconds *the chickenpox literally disappeared from her friend's face*! Then, the teacher prayed for the coordinator and the same thing happened! After that, they declared healing over the room, calling down Heaven to kick out the sickness in Jesus' name. Within days there were no new cases at the center, and within two weeks the chickenpox was gone, allowing the children who'd had it and were now healed to return.

This experience highlights the importance of being carriers of the presence of God. We must have a close relationship with Him and walk in the authority He has given us. Not all things are as they seem. We should always ask Him first and depend on Him in every situation. Reflect on your life and think of areas in which you could depend on Him more, then hand those areas over to Him.

JESUS HEALS A SHAMAN

A miraculous healing that was just as dramatic occurred through prayer over the life of a shaman of an indigenous tribe living in our neighborhood. Since 1964, Colombia has been in a civil war that has left around ten percent of its population as displaced refugees of the conflict. The rebel groups have occupied and operated in remote places in the jungles and mountains of Colombia where these indigenous tribes live. These precious people are very vulnerable to the overwhelming force of rebels with modern weaponry, causing them to flee to cities seeking refuge.

In this way, about two hundred and fifty members of the Embera Katio tribe moved into the inner-city slums near the children's center. This tribe sticks together, trying not to mix with other people. That's why it was surprising when they came to the children's center one day to sign their children up for the preschool program. They had been watching us for a long time and had decided we were worthy of taking care of their children. They also invited me to their slum housing to meet their tribal leaders. What an honor!

The entire group of Embera Katios in our neighborhood lived in two separate slum buildings, each three stories tall with narrow stairways. Visiting them was a surreal experience, as if stepping into a jungle village. No sooner had I climbed halfway up the narrow staircase when

I was mobbed by naked indigenous children who were laughing and running up and down the stairs. I noticed smoke and the smell of burning wood coming from several rooms, as if they had been cooking with a campfire on the floor.

Most of the shirtless and barefoot men and women were doing chores, while a few rested in homemade hammocks strewn across a balcony. I greeted the tribal leaders, family leaders, and the shaman. After spending some time getting to know them, I invited them to a meeting at the center a few days later during which we planned to help them start up their own micro-businesses. As I descended the stairway to leave, the children smiled and waved at me.

At the meeting later that week, the shaman arrived with a strained look on his face and mentioned that he was suffering from a painful migraine. This was the same week we were hosting a Missions Intensive school, and some of these students happened to be in the room with us.

I asked the shaman if we could pray for him and he agreed. Seizing the opportunity, I asked two young Missions Intensive students to pray for him and following their quick prayer his migraine disappeared! The shaman asked if they could pray for his chronic neck pain, and to his astonishment within seconds it was also healed in Jesus' name! Stunned at the miraculous relief from his pain, he asked how this had happened.

We explained that Jesus is God of the universe, and it was His love and authority that healed the shaman. Jesus loved him and cared about the details of his life. He wanted to be part of the shaman's life. The shaman told the other Emberas that Jesus was real and had healed him! He left that day changed in many ways. Even more important, he and many others recognized that the name of Jesus is greater than any other name.

CONCLUSION

The shaman and the brave ex-witch in these stories had only known one power throughout their lives - a wicked power. They loved their families and were trying the best they could to protect them. It wasn't until they met someone who would not judge them, but instead would step out, take a risk, and show them a different and better way - the way of Jesus - that they found true protection and were set free.

Jesus is real and His power is real. He is above every other power, including that of the enemy. When His light shines, there is no one and nothing that can put it out. He is never scared or intimidated, and He always knows what to do. We just need to lean on Him and trust that He will take action as we take faith-filled steps. We must be confident that He will intervene and answer our prayers. He breaks down every barrier and argument anyone could bring against Him.

This dark world needs His light now more than ever, and He's chosen ordinary people like you and me to be living light bulbs!

We don't know the details of the spiritual forces of darkness behind the chickenpox breakout, but we *do* know that it was much more than just a "coincidence." Was it some specific witchcraft purported by occult leaders in the area, or part of some other wicked scheme? How did it gain access and a foothold at the center? We don't know and we don't care. We just keep our focus on the One who understands everything and has the solution.

When Jesus is our focus, our refuge, our rescuer, and our defender in times of need, the stage is set for Him to "show up." He is a trustworthy and faithful Friend Who comes through when all else fails. When He brings the light, the darkness flees. This dark world needs His light now more than ever, and He's chosen ordinary people like you and me to be living light bulbs! Let's allow our lights to shine!

ACTION CHALLENGE

1. Think about a dark situation in your life or the lives of those close to you. Ask God to show you how to let light into that situation, and then take steps of faith and action to follow God's leading.

2. Take a moment to think about a place in which you might feel darkness or wickedness. This could be a school, an office, a home, a store, a neighborhood, etc. Ask God to go with you the next time you are there, and to shine His light through you in that place. Just before entering, take a moment to completely focus on Jesus and His presence in and around you.

3. Journal about your thoughts and experiences.

Chapter Fourteen

MANNA IN MEDELLÍN

*"Trust in the Lord with all your heart and lean
not on your own understanding; in all your
ways submit to him, and he will make your
paths straight" (NIV, Proverbs 3:5-6).*

Did you ever hear the phrase, "The safest place on earth is to be in the will of God?" We know by experience this is true! As we have followed Him into dangerous places and situations, desiring not only that He move in our lives but also in the lives of those to whom we minister, He has never let us down. Many of the children we minister to have been horribly abused and have witnessed the power of the enemy in such terrible ways that only a tangible breakthrough miracle can take their focus off of wickedness and put it onto God. Short of this, nothing else will do!

The stories in this chapter demonstrate God's unfailing love manifested when we trust Him in every situation, no matter how difficult. We believe these stories will inspire you to put your faith into action and follow Jesus wherever He leads.

THE HONEYMOON IS OVER

Our first assignment in Colombia was to serve as Executive Directors of a children's center in a drug-ridden neighborhood decimated by homelessness, prostitution, poverty, and violence. About two weeks into the job a serious situation developed. The mother of a three-year-old boy in our program sought us out and explained that a man in a dangerous gang had sexually abused her son. She demanded we not call the police under any circumstances because the perpetrator was a member of a dangerous paramilitary mafia group composed of killers and drug traffickers. Our call would put many lives at risk.

The leader of the gang was the boy's grandfather, and the mother herself was involved in the trafficking and abuse of drugs. She warned that if our foundation were to denounce this abuse, the gang would find out and take revenge by killing all of our staff members. The director of another foundation we partnered with raced over for an emergency meeting as soon as he heard the news. Knowing the extreme danger we were in, he also warned us not to call the police about this case.

Law enforcement and prosecution in Colombia are not as straightforward as we might hope or expect. There is a police presence, but they rarely protect people from the most dangerous criminals. There is a judicial system, but offenders are frequently not brought to justice for terrible crimes committed. When there's a threat from powerful criminals, people often have little recourse except to run into hiding for the rest of their lives. The director warned me not to denounce this heinous act given that I was a tall, white American who would be easy to find. He stressed that my wife and kids would be in grave danger of being killed as well.

Wow…what a welcome to Colombia! When a missionary moves to another culture, there are known phases of cultural adjustment: honeymoon, crisis/frustration, adjustment, and acceptance. In the honeymoon phase everything is exciting and new. After that, culture shock hits like a bag of bricks and the missionary is tempted to want to go home. If they hang in there, not giving in to the temptation to run back to their home culture, adjustment begins to happen. This eventually results in acceptance of this new way of life as "normal." Needless to say, our honeymoon period had come to a screaming halt just a few weeks after our arrival! As we nervously joked at the time, "We're *definitely* not in Kansas anymore!"

LIFE OR DEATH

I had a dilemma on my hands. If I didn't report this to the police, the foundation and I would both be considered accomplices to this grave offense. Not reporting sexual abuse of a minor is, and should be, a crime. If I reported it, however, my family and I would likely be murdered along with the other employees in the foundation we had just begun to direct. Had God moved mountains and performed miracles to bring us to Colombia, just to allow us to die within the first few weeks?

To me, not reporting this would be like lying. Could we start our work as missionaries to the poor by covering up a terrible crime? How would God bless that? If we put ourselves in God's hands by doing the right thing, would He protect us and allow us to live? If we reported it, would our lives have been a waste, being murdered just weeks after coming to Colombia? But if we were to acquiesce to the lie, how could we ever move forward with integrity? I shuddered at the mere thought of that option. I'd much rather do the right thing and take the chance of dying than to move ahead based on a lie.

That evening we called our intercessors and after some time together in prayer determined that I would go in the next day and call the police myself regardless of the consequences. However, we begged God to perform a miracle so this wouldn't be necessary, but so that justice would still be served.

A CHANGE OF HEART

When I arrived at the center at 8:00 am the next morning, I was stunned to find the mother of the abused child entering close behind me. The day before, she had outright refused to call the police out of fear for her life and for her family. However, she now shared that she'd called the police herself the night prior, *while we were interceding*, even though she worried they would incriminate her for involvement in drug trafficking.

We were able to find specialized psychological and material aid and protection for the mother and small boy, to help them begin the healing process. What a miracle! God had extended His mighty hand and protected us!

Have you ever faced a hopeless situation in which you could see no way out? Sometimes we can feel that no matter what we do or how hard we try, we're still thrown to the ground and unable to get up. While we're on the ground, we realize all of our human effort can't help us. Many times other people can't help us either.

It is when we are alone on the ground and feeling defeated that there is only one way to look, and that is *up*! Opening our eyes with our backs to the ground, we find ourselves looking up toward Heaven, and that is where our help comes from! When our gaze turns to Him, everything changes, because He is the God of miracles and wonders.

When King David wrote Psalm 77, he was often in that same position, with his back on the ground, alone and hopeless. It is there that he found the God of miracles! He wrote, "You are the God who performs miracles; you display your power among the peoples" (*NIV*, Psalm 77:14). It is in that same place where we have found Him, and where you will also find Him.

This next story results from looking to Heaven for help in a situation that was impossible to fix in our human strength. When we didn't know what else to do, we decided to believe that God's Word, the Bible, is not fiction but fact, and that the same miracles recorded in it can happen today if we just step out in faith.

FOOD FROM HEAVEN

In a neighborhood where so many people go hungry, the children's center was feeding up to two hundred children five days a week, providing significant help to the families. However, during times of prayer many of the children would all have the same petition. They would start by giving thanks to God for their food, but then cry out to Him to feed their parents and siblings, who were often suffering from hunger. We had no extra funds to feed and sustain entire families, so our teachers decided to show the children how to pray faith-filled prophetic prayers.

They explained to the children how the Israelites had been hungry in the wilderness and had called out to God, Who responded with manna sent from Heaven. The teachers encouraged these preschool children that if there was no food in the house, they should go to the kitchen, pull out the empty pots and pans, lay their hands on them, and ask God to fill them.

The kids went home for the weekend, and on Monday morning several perplexed mothers came in to talk to the teachers. One said, "The craziest thing happened this weekend! When my daughter asked what was for dinner, I told her we had no food in the house. She then ran to the kitchen, pulled out the pots and pans, put her hands on them, and prayed. A few minutes later there was a knock on the door. When we answered, it was a neighbor who had brought groceries for us! What happened here on Friday? What did you tell my daughter to do?"

Another mother related how, after her young child had prayed for the pots and pans, the mother had gone to sell candy on the street. As she was walking home afterward, not having sold any candy, someone handed her a bag of groceries for her family. In this neighborhood people have very little resources and typically don't trust each other. and giving a gift such as groceries is extremely rare. Other moms had similar stories of their child's faith and God's miraculous provision.

During that season, the faith of small children saved their families from going hungry. God moved mightily just as in the days of freeing the Israelites from their bondage in Egypt. This story proves that He still moves His mighty arm for those children who call out to Him in faith.

CONCLUSION

Have you ever been in a situation in which there seems to be no way out, just as we felt in the two stories above? The

> *The amazing thing is that no matter how impossible a situation seems, God is able to make a way where no other exists.*

amazing thing is that no matter how impossible a situation seems, God is able to make a way where no other exists. That's why He's sometimes called the "Waymaker." He makes streams of water in the desert and causes green plants to bloom there. He's the One who makes water come out of rocks, bread fall from Heaven, and divides the sea so you can walk through. The most important part is that God sent the payment for your sin, which only He could pay.

Do you realize it's often not until we are backed into a corner without hope and with no escape that we turn our attention to Him? It's in these times when there is no "Plan B" and all hope is lost that we turn to Him for help. Then He breaks through our problems and gives us a Heavenly solution. However, He was waiting to do this long before we were at the end of our rope!

Breakthrough is a military term which means breaking through a barrier and making a way where there was none. This is an excellent description of our God. His actions show Him to be the "God of the

Breakthrough," and we live our lives in a spiritual battlefield, running into barriers that only He can bring down. Our job is to turn to Him for help and guidance throughout our day, not only when we are at the end of our own resources!

I challenge you to raise your faith to a new level today. Trust Him not only with the specific barrier you are facing right now, but also with all of your future unseen needs in a distant sea of uncertainty. I cannot promise that He will take away all your trouble. I can promise, however, that if you trust and follow Him, He will bring you into a deep inner peace and keep you there, regardless of whether He takes the storm away or allows you to go through it with Him by your side.

ACTION CHALLENGE

1. Take a moment and evaluate the areas of your life in which you are not fully trusting God. Write down a few practical steps you can take this week in order to begin trusting God completely in these areas of your life.
2. Take a moment to pray and hand these areas over to God, giving Him complete authority to do whatever He wants in your situation.
3. Keep track of your prayers and His responses in your journal.

Chapter Fifteen

A PSALM, THOUSANDS OF ANGELS, AND A FEW DEMONS

*"Whoever dwells in the shelter of the Most High will rest
in the shadow of the Almighty" (NIV, Psalm 91:1).*

This true story explains what happened to a woman who had attended a church in Bogotá. One Saturday night the preacher spoke on the supernatural protection found in Psalm 91. While walking home after the service, she noticed a suspicious man following her. Afraid he would rob her or do something worse, with a racing heart she began to pray and then to run. The man took off after her, less than half a block behind and closing in quickly. She knew she couldn't outrun him and there was no one around to help.

REAL PROTECTION

With his footsteps close behind her, she whipped around a corner. Putting all her faith in God, she crouched down in a ball next to a wall and prayed, "Cover me with your feathers, Lord!" As the man turned the corner, he miraculously ran right past her and disappeared into the darkness ahead. The woman heaved a great sigh of relief and uttered a prayer of thanks to God for covering her with His feathers and making her "invisible" to the man chasing her.

Do you desire supernatural protection in your life? Do you want to live in peace and safety, far from worry and fear? Then you should not only make Psalm 91 part of your life, but also make your life part of Psalm 91! This chapter of the Bible has guided and encouraged us so much that we want to share this amazing supernatural key with you. We believe it will change your life!

VERSE 1: DWELLING = RESTING

Psalm 91 begins by saying, "Whoever dwells in the shelter of the Most High will rest in the shadow of the Almighty" (*NIV*, Psalm 91:1). Verse one holds the key to everything that comes after it. The promises of Psalm 91 are not for everyone. They are only for those who live (dwell) in the shelter that God provides for them. That shelter is His presence. To be in His presence means you must abide and remain in Him.

Jesus says, "Remain in me, as I also remain in you. No branch can bear fruit by itself; it must remain in the vine. Neither can you bear fruit unless you remain in me" (*NIV*, John 15:4). Those who live in and out of His presence will find rest in His covering (shadow).

VERSE 2: TRUSTING IN GOD

Verse 2 says, "I will say of the Lord, 'He is my refuge and my fortress, my God, in whom I trust'" (*NIV*, Psalm 91:2). Where do you find refuge when things get tough? Many people take refuge in food, drink, drugs, or some type of sexual release outside the bond of marriage. For those who practice being in the presence of God minute by minute and day by day it will be natural to turn to Him in times of trouble or when they are tired and discouraged. Since they have learned to trust God by spending time with Him, it will be normal for them to find their refuge in Him.

Finding our refuge in God in the small things trains us to run to Him as our refuge and fortress when we encounter big problems. Being in His presence is simply being aware of Him throughout the day. It's having a constant, quiet conversation with God, asking Him questions and listening. It's sitting with Him, feeling content in showering your love on Him as He showers His love on you.

In the past, I've been confronted with tough situations that have left me feeling paralyzed, worn out, and filled with negative emotions such as fear, despair, disappointment, and uncertainty. In those times, I've fallen to the ground crying out to God, telling Him I *cannot* and *will not* get up until He comes and lifts me up Himself. I've put all of my affection and attention on Jesus until He comes and breaks off the invisible accusatory enemies trying to tear me down.

God has *never* failed to rescue me in times like these. He always comes, bringing His peace, wisdom, correction, and rest. Many times it feels as if a peaceful white sheet glides down from Heaven to cover me, calming my emotions and enabling me to focus on Him. This Shelter, which is none other than God, has always been a faithful refuge for me. I trust Him even when He doesn't reveal the reason for the storm I'm in or the pain I'm feeling. I need not understand why certain things happen. I just need to trust my faithful Friend as a child trusts their parents.

VERSE 3: HE SAVES YOU

The third verse says, "Surely he will save you from the fowler's snare and from the deadly pestilence" (*NIV*, Psalm 91:3). A snare is a trap, and the fowler (hunter) is the enemy who has set many spiritual traps to keep you in bondage to sin and suffering. This verse is saying that it's a sure thing God will save you. He will not only protect you from deceitful traps but also free you from traps into which you have already fallen.

Your Heavenly Father knows that you will fall sometimes. He is gracious enough to even save you from the traps you fall into all by yourself, so throw all shame and regret behind you. Get rid of those feelings of being a failure and begin to dwell and abide in His presence. Trust that He will save you from the current trap you are in and any that may follow. He will provide a way out!

A deadly pestilence is an invisible threat that is hard to stop, such as an epidemic disease or virus. We live in a world in which deadly viruses such as Ebola, coronavirus, and SARS are popping up everywhere. We must believe that the Heavenly Father will save us from these plagues and those still to come. We must trust Him, believe Him, and declare what He says over our lives in this verse.

VERSE 4: HE COVERS YOU

Psalm 91:4 says, "He will cover you with his feathers, and under his wings you will find refuge; his faithfulness will be your shield and rampart" (*NIV*, Psalm 91:4). When there's a threat to a mother hen's little chicks, she spreads out her wings and calls them to herself. Sometimes she does this because she sees an eagle in the sky who could prey on her chicks. Other times she might just want to shelter them from the rain.

Just like God, she provides the shelter and calls her children to come close. However, the little chicks must trust her call and run to her. The chicks have the responsibility to act. They must place themselves underneath her spread-out wings, or they will be in danger. In the same way we must run to God for our refuge, intentionally placing ourselves under His wings.

Our positioning is not physical like the chicks going to their mother, but a positioning of the heart. When disaster hits, if we first seek refuge in God rather than making Him our last choice, we will find peace in the midst of the storm.

Jesus used the analogy of a mother hen when He met with resistance to His ministry. He said, "Jerusalem, Jerusalem...how often I have longed to gather your children together, as a hen gathers her chicks under her wings, and you were not willing" (*NIV*, Luke 13:34). Let's not be like the people about which Jesus was talking. Instead, let's position our hearts and attitudes to look to Him first, whether in great need or great abundance, regardless of the circumstances.

As missionaries working in a neighborhood filled with violence, the occult, drugs, and extreme poverty, there are few options available other than God's miraculous intervention. We have the privilege of having only "Plan A," which is, *God, if You don't move, we are in big trouble. You are our only hope! We don't have a "Plan B"!*

His faithfulness protects us as a shield and rampart. A rampart is a wide defensive wall erected around castles or cities in ancient times. The top of the wall is wide enough to walk on, and some are several meters wide. God is that wall which protects us from all the outside influences and attacks. His shield protects us from the arrows of doubt and accusation shot by the enemy.

VERSE 5: YOU WILL NOT FEAR

Psalm 91:5 says, "You will not fear the terror of night, nor the arrow that flies by day" (*NIV*, Psalm 91:5). The terror of the night is anything that could happen in your worst fears at night. They used arrows in Old Testament times, while today we have bullets, bombs, and missiles. His peace protects our minds from fear and very real and horrible dangers.

VERSE 6: THE PLAGUE WILL NOT TOUCH YOU

Psalm 91:6-8 says, "nor the pestilence that stalks in the darkness, nor the plague that destroys at midday. A thousand may fall at your side, ten thousand at your right hand, but it will not come near you. You will only observe with your eyes and see the punishment of the wicked" (*NIV*, Psalm 91:6-8). Pestilence and plagues can attack without warning at any hour of the day or night. This verse urges us not to be afraid even when people are dying around you. That is *not* for you! You are protected. Don't focus on the tragedy and death, but on the mighty hand of God stretched out to cover you.

VERSE 9: NO HARM WILL COME NEAR YOUR HOME

Psalm 91:9 says, "If you say, 'The Lord is my refuge,' and you make the Most High your dwelling, no harm will overtake you, no disaster will come near your tent" (*NIV*, Psalm 91:9). This is a rephrasing of verse one. There is a condition you must meet to receive God's amazing protection and blessing. You must declare, trust, and believe in your innermost being, "The Lord is my refuge." You must make Him your dwelling.

Psalm 91:9a says, "no harm will overtake you" (*NIV*, Psalm 91:9a). This means that although you may run into harm, it will not be victorious over you. Most people don't live in tents anymore, but rather houses, so the verse declares that no disaster will come near your house. Declare it and believe it!

VERSE 11-12: HE WILL PROTECT YOU

Psalm 91:11-12 says, "For he will command his angels concerning you to guard you in all your ways; they will lift you up in their hands, so that you will not strike your foot against a stone" (*NIV*, Psalm 91:11-12). No harm will overtake you and no disaster will come near you because in the unseen realm God has positioned angels all around you. Though you may not see them, they are there protecting you at all times!

When I used to pray about angels lifting us up in their hands, I'd imagine them around my family protecting us, and I'd believe in my heart that they were there. However, it wasn't until I saw their miraculous intervention with my son Gabriel that this verse came to life for me. I then realized that my praying and declaring this Psalm was not in vain but had expressed a reality we rarely perceive.

GABRIEL'S ANGEL

One weekend we took our kids to beautiful hot springs in the Colombian mountainside several hours outside of the city. The cabin we stayed in had a large loft about nine and a half feet above the hard concrete floor, and it was accessed by a narrow ladder. Our four-year-old son Gabriel was excited to sleep in the loft that night so we let him, not thinking of the potential danger. With the lights off the room was pitch black. You couldn't even see your hand in front of your face. Not thinking to turn the bathroom light on, we slept in utter darkness.

In the middle of the night I awoke and felt a sudden urge to pray. As I did, I had a vision of Jacob's ladder with angels descending and ascending. Jesus was standing halfway up the ladder, looking at the loft. At that very moment I heard Gabe's body falling from the loft and landing with a thud on the hard concrete floor. I knew that falling from a height of over nine feet onto a cement floor could cause head trauma, brain damage, or even break a person's neck or back, rendering one paralyzed for life.

Calling out to Gabe but hearing no answer, I stumbled over in the dark and found him. Praying for healing and concerned that Gabe wasn't making any noise, I called for Jen to awaken and turn on the light. From a fall like that he should at least be crying or whimpering. When Jen turned on the lights I discovered why.

Helping him to his feet, I found Gabe calm and relaxed. He had no broken bones or head trauma. He wasn't bleeding, nor was he frightened or hurt. The only sign of his fall was a small scratch on his side, which came from grazing the corner of a table.

He'd gotten up to go to the bathroom in the night, and when he flipped his legs over the side where he thought the ladder should be, his feet met with open space and he fell. I believe angels came down from the ladder in my vision to keep Gabe from "stubbing his foot on a stone," let alone his head and entire body. This is not the only time we have witnessed divine angelic intervention to protect his life.

THE WARRIOR ANGEL

We understand the concept of guardian angels, but it doesn't seem real until you witness one guarding you and your entire family. The thin veil that separates the seen from the unseen has often been removed for our son Alex who shares with us details of God's angels at work as he sees them.

For a period when our children were younger, almost every night someone in our house would have a nightmare. It seemed like a constant attack. Fed up one night with these attacks, I decided to declare Psalm 91 over my family before we all went to sleep. Our three bedrooms are close to each other, with the girls right across the hall from the boys.

After the kids crawled into their beds, I stood between the two bedrooms, extended my arms out toward each one, and began to declare Psalm 91. Seconds into the prayer, my ten-year-old son Alex interrupted me, urging, "Dad...Dad..." A bit annoyed at the interruption, I responded, "Hold on, I'm praying. Just wait." After praying, I asked Alex what he'd wanted to say.

He replied, "Dad, when you began to pray, I saw a big angel appear right behind you. He was a bright golden color and had armor all over that was shining. He wore a helmet, and a sword was hanging on his belt. He was strong and intense, and had a bow and arrow drawn. His eyes were narrowed and searching back and forth for someone to shoot. I also saw enormous bats with three-meter wingspans outside our house trying to get in, but they couldn't because the angel wouldn't let them!"

The God of the angel armies had sent His angelic troops to protect us, and after that night, the nightmares left! Every one of God's promises are powerful and true for those who abide in Him.

VERSE 13: YOU WILL TREAD ON DEMONS

Psalm 91:13 says, "You will tread on the lion and the cobra; you will trample the great lion and the serpent" (*NIV*, Psalm 91:13). In this verse, lions and serpents refer to demons. Jesus has delegated to us the authority to cast out demons, ward off attacks, and free the oppressed.

VERSE 14: HE WILL RESCUE YOU

Psalm 91:14 says, "'Because he loves me,' says the Lord, 'I will rescue him; I will protect him, for he acknowledges my name'" (*NIV*, Psalm 91:14). The Heavenly Father protects and rescues those who love Him and who seek Him throughout their day. He protects those who abide in Him, acknowledging Him in everything they do.

VERSE 15: HE WILL DELIVER YOU

Psalm 91:15-16 says, "He will call on me, and I will answer him; I will be with him in trouble, I will deliver him and honor him. With long life I will satisfy him and show him my salvation" (*NIV*, Psalm 91:15-16). These last two verses show God's delight with the person who delights in Him, who develops a friendship with God and walks in His presence. Today is the day to seek God with all your heart. Call out to Him and He will answer you!

> *Every one of God's promises are powerful and true for those who abide in Him.*

THE CURSED HOUSE

We experienced this protection when we moved into our first apartment in Colombia. Part of a condominium complex of about eighty apartments, it was perfect for our family of five. We were thrilled that it was right next to the playground so we could monitor our three small children as they played outside. The previous renter had left several large, bulky, hanging tropical plants on the patio. Since we didn't have much to decorate with at first, it seemed fine to just leave them there.

Several days after moving in, a few of our Colombian neighbors stopped by and asked how we "felt" in the apartment. We were thrilled to be living in such an agreeable place and thankful to God that it was in a safe neighborhood, and we answered that we felt great. Every now and then various neighbors would continue to stop by and ask, "So, how do you feel in the house?" or "Is everything okay there?" The roof leaked when it rained, but that didn't seem to be the answer they were seeking. I wondered why they kept asking, as we always told them that everything was fine.

After a year of living in the house, there was a knock on the door one morning. A lady we had never seen before explained that she had rented the house a few years back and had come to retrieve the plants she'd left on the porch. Seconds later, a Christian neighbor showed up at the door, keeping a close eye on the mysterious lady and peppering her with questions. The lady seemed nervous and in a hurry to get her plants and leave, and within minutes of her arrival she and her plants were gone.

As soon as she left, I looked at our friend and asked, "What was that all about?" She told us that the past three tenants in our apartment had all moved out with little notice, saying evil spirits had haunted the house. That's why the apartment had been available and at such a good price. The owner had been losing money because of all the weird paranormal things that were happening to his tenants.

Our friend explained that the mysterious lady had expressed complaints against the owner and vowed to put a curse on the apartment to drive all future tenants out. It is common here for people in the occult to hide ritual objects carrying spells and curses in the dirt of potted plants, and I believe this is what happened. Once she realized the curse had no effect on our family, she came back to retrieve her property and occult objects.

We now understood why everyone was asking how we "felt" in the house. They didn't want to say the house was haunted yet were perplexed as to why the curse did not have any effect on us. God's protection from this curse reminded me of the book of Proverbs, which says, "Like a fluttering sparrow or a darting swallow, an undeserved curse does not come to rest" (*NIV*, Proverbs 26:2).

I later asked the Holy Spirit if there were any other occult objects in our house, and if so, to show me their location so we could remove them. I felt led to our second-floor bathroom and sensed I should take the cover off of the water tank of the toilet. The inside of the old tank was mildewy-brown, so it was hard to see to the bottom. When I put my hand in and felt around, I discovered an object at the bottom of the tank. Pulling it out, I saw to my surprise that it was a ghostly white figure with a twisting tail instead of feet.

I prayed the blood of Jesus over the object, cancelled the assignment of the enemy in Jesus' name, and threw it away. God's faithfulness in leading me to the exact spot where the occult object was hidden was an amazing example of the deliverance and protection available to us when we abide in God.

CONCLUSION

Psalm 91 describes the angelic protection of God. It promises, "For he will command his angels concerning you to guard you in all your ways; they will lift you up in their hands, so that you will not strike your foot against a stone" (*NIV*, Psalm 91:11-12). Although I rarely see angels, I can sense their presence and know they are carrying out His promises, which include this verse! We are so thankful that God is faithful and fulfills His Word. He is there to lead us and answer our prayers when we ask. As it says in Matthew, "Ask and it will be given to you; seek and you will find" (*NIV*, Matthew 7:7a). I asked and He answered. Trust that He'll do the same for you!

I don't know the issues, dangers, or troubles you may be facing right now. However, I do know that a life given over to Jesus and abiding in Him is one in which He will intervene. I can't promise that everything will go the way you think it should, because you may not understand what is best for your life. However, I can

There is no better refuge for your life than to be in the arms of Jesus.

guarantee that His peace will be with you. There is no better refuge for your life than to be in the arms of Jesus. Trust Him with all of your heart! He will come through for you!

ACTION CHALLENGE

PSALM 91 DECLARATION

I invite you to declare Psalm 91 over yourself, your family, and your home. Read the declarations below out loud and with resolution:

- I declare that I live and abide in the Presence of God. He is my shelter and I am at rest in His presence. Yahweh is my refuge and my fortress. I trust in Him.
- He will save me from all the enemy's traps and from deadly diseases.
- He covers me with His Presence, and I find refuge under His wings.
- His faithfulness is my shield and rampart.
- I will not fear the terror of the night, nor the bullets that fly in the day, nor the pestilence that stalks in the darkness, nor the plague that destroys at midday.
- Thousands may fall at my side, ten thousand at my right hand, but disaster will not come near me.
- I make the Most High my home. He is my refuge so no harm will come to me and no disaster will come near my house.
- God commands His angels to protect and guard me in all my ways. They lift me up in their hands, so I won't even trip.
- Jesus gives me authority over demons and all their weapons.
- Because I love God, He will rescue me.
- God protects me because I acknowledge His name.
- When I call, Jesus answers.
- He will be with me in trouble, He will deliver me and honor me, and show me His salvation.

Chapter Sixteen

BOGOTÁ, MOZAMBIQUE, AND A JOURNEY TOWARD THE EXTRAORDINARY

"For I am convinced that neither death nor life, neither angels nor demons, neither the present nor the future, nor any powers, neither height nor depth, nor anything else in all creation, will be able to separate us from the love of God that is in Christ Jesus our Lord" (NIV, Romans 8:38-39).

Sure...our dream was to be missionaries in Colombia, but we'd visited the country only once before and had no idea how to get that dream off the ground. We brought all this up with our pastors, who agreed we should take a few survey trips to confirm the call and get a better idea of where we would go and what we might do.

Having always loved Youth With a Mission because of their radical dependence on the Holy Spirit, we started there. After contacting several of their missionary bases in Latin America, we decided to visit Steve and Evie Bartel, directors of an amazing ministry to street children in Bogotá, Colombia, which they had begun in the early 1980s.

THE AUDIBLE VOICE

Jen and I arrived in Bogotá a few weeks later, excited to find out what God had in store for us. As we talked with Steve that first afternoon, I sat mesmerized as he shared how just before his graduation from college, he'd heard God's *audible voice* calling him into a ministry to street children. Steve knew it had been God speaking, because as a young child street kids had beaten him up and stolen his bike. In his mind they were "gamines," a derogatory slang word for street children, and without a doubt the last people on earth to which Steve wanted to minister! However, God made His message to Steve clear by audibly using that very word: "gamines."

God also told him he was to marry a classmate and close friend before going to Colombia, and that she would share his desire to care for these street children in Bogotá. Since Steve didn't want to minister to street kids, he told nobody about the words God had spoken to him. However, a few days later, his Mexican-American friend Evie came to his room and asked if he would like to raise a dozen street kids with her in Bogotá. They married and moved to Colombia to start a ministry which has been wonderfully successful in restoring and helping hundreds of street children, delivering them from a tragic life on the streets.

DOES GOD STILL SPEAK?

As I stood there listening to Steve, a monumental struggle was taking place within me. At that point there were several Christian leaders in my life who doubted that God still speaks or gives clear and pertinent direction to people today. However, the fruit in Steve's life was undeniable. God had given him great faith and the obedience to do something he did not want to do in and of himself. God's audible word had catapulted Steve into a lifelong journey of living by faith, pleasing God, and starting a highly successful and impactful ministry.

That ministry has grown throughout the years to include the formation of grade schools, a strong Youth With A Mission (YWAM) mission base, a ministry training program that reproduces their model for others around the world, the restoration of street children who would otherwise be lost forever, and many souls brought to salvation through Jesus Christ. In addition, he had a beautiful large family and a joyous, fulfilling marriage!

I decided that if these blessings were the result of hearing God's voice, I needed to hear His voice too! Although to date I haven't had the experience of hearing God's *audible* voice while awake (I *have* heard what I believe was His audible voice in a dream), throughout the years He has confirmed my destiny and calling through many experiences, including hearing His "still small voice." Though not audible, it may as well have been so, considering its incredible impact on my life!

WHERE DO WE GO?

After that trip, another YWAM base caught our attention, this one started by a Colombian in San Salvador, the capital of El Salvador. The great need, obvious poverty, and overabundance of street children in this city broke our hearts. As much as we wanted to love and care for every one of them, we now began to realize that there was desperate need everywhere...Colombia, El Salvador, Brazil...and in all of Central and South America!

This created quite a dilemma. If there was need everywhere, how on earth were we to decide where to go? At the YWAM base in San Salvador we'd read an inspirational book written by YWAM founder Loren Cunningham called *Is That Really You, God?* (Cunningham, 1984)[xiv]. In it, Cunningham shares the story about how God's still small voice had led him step by step through the creation of one of the largest and most impactful missions agencies and Christian youth movements in the world!

We were desperate for God's guidance and direction regarding this dramatic change in our lives, so we spent the last day in San Salvador in fasting and prayer, crying out to God and asking where He wanted us to serve. We didn't want to make a mistake, choosing a place based on our emotions instead of God's will. Although we felt very close to Him that day, we did not hear Him the way we thought He'd speak. A bit disappointed, we ended our day of fasting and prayer with no clear direction from God.

He did speak to us, but not in the timing or manner we expected, and certainly not with the answer for which we were hoping. It wasn't until the following day while walking through the Houston airport that God caught us by surprise, stopping us in our tracks as if we had bumped into an invisible wall. We didn't hear an audible voice, yet there was an inner voice, or thoughts that were not ours, that said, "You two have been very focused on the poor children. Don't you think it would be better to focus on *Me*?"

ARMS WRAPPED AROUND THE WAIST OF JESUS

This blindsided us, because we had never considered that our focus might be misplaced. Looking back to the first trip to Cartagena in 1995 in which we'd seen the small child sleeping in a paper bag on the street, God had been softening and breaking our hearts for the orphans, street children, and pre-street children in Latin America who were suffering horrific atrocities with no one to love or protect them. Most of these children had been deprived of love for the entirety of their young lives and had no idea of what true love was, much less of Jesus' great love for them.

We recognized that our entire focus *was* on these poor children and on answering the question of where we should start serving as missionaries. Now God was encouraging us to switch our greatest focus and pursuit to Him, trusting that He would take care of all the kids and the problems that were too big for us. He was teaching us that everything else must be secondary to our connectedness to Jesus, and that our hopes, dreams, protection, and future destination are all found in and through our connectedness to Him. This was the start of a pursuit of the only One who really matters, and a turning point from focusing on the "ministry" to focusing on the amazing King of kings.

We are made complete only in Jesus, and nothing matters more than our connectedness with Him. Even today it is our greatest need, our greatest desire, and our greatest pleasure. Right there in the airport we repented for not having kept Jesus at the center of everything. We gave Him the burden we felt for the street children and pre-street children in all of Latin America, and we felt Him give us His joy and peace in return.

It was as if He were saying, "If your only desire is for more of Me, it doesn't matter where I send you. That way, no matter where you are, you will be sold-out worshipers in love with Me, and I will be Myself and provide everything you need...and more."

In the airport I had a vision in which I felt like a little child with my arms wrapped around Jesus' waist, holding on as hard as I could. With my heart in this position of complete surrender I knew that as long as I held on like this to my Jesus, I would go wherever He went, and would end up just where He wanted me to be.

Once the question changed from where we would land in South America to how close to Father God we would be when and if we did, it no longer seemed as important if we ever even got there. The most important thing became connectedness with our Heavenly Father.

This would help us in the years to come, because whether the overall ministry is going well or not, Jesus is always our focus. It doesn't matter if we have an outstanding day or a horrible one, whether a project is successful or doesn't go as planned. He is always our constant, remaining at the center of everything we do. He roots us and keeps us stable through the storms. When there is a victory, we celebrate it with

Him. He is where we begin and end, and only in Him do we find our purpose, help, and refuge.

MIRACLES IN MOZAMBIQUE

Since our best plan was to be YWAM missionaries, partnering with one of their ministries seemed an obvious choice. Apart from being the largest missions agency in the world, YWAM is decentralized, offering missionaries incredible flexibility. In addition, the organization values the guidance of the Holy Spirit. To become more familiar with their missionary model, we read some books written by current YWAM missionaries.

We soon stumbled across a book called *Always Enough* (Baker, 2003)[xv] written by Heidi and Rolland Baker, experienced missionaries serving in Mozambique, Africa. For decades they have loved and ministered to thousands of orphans forgotten by society, and their labor of love continues to this day. *Always Enough* transformed my life. It was impossible to read two pages without my being so tangibly touched by God that tears flowed as my love and faith in Him were reignited.

In particular, the unique way their team evangelizes the lost villages in the jungles of Africa impacted me. Most of the villages are populated by animistic Muslims whose religious leaders are called imams. The Baker's ministry team will contact the local imam asking for permission to show the "Jesus" film and share about Him. The imam often gives them permission but warns that the villagers may stone the team after hearing about Jesus.

Among the missionaries are children from their orphanage, and after showing the film, the team asks for all the deaf villagers to come forward. The children pray for Jesus to restore the deaf villagers' hearing, and most or all of the deaf are healed within minutes! Jumping up and down in astonishment and joy, the imams then begin praising Jesus and saying that their god has done nothing like that. They then encourage the villagers to make Jesus their God, and an entire village comes to Jesus overnight with the once-imam as their new pastor!

These stories brought me to tears because I could feel the tangible love of Jesus wanting to gather in all of His children. They also frustrated me, because I knew I had missed the great blessing of truly believing that through Jesus *all things are possible*. If children praying in Jesus' name can bring incredible healing and transformation, leading entire villages to God in just one day, *what else* is God able to release through us?

It reminded me of all that Jesus is and what He accomplished by dying. He died that we might live! He came to bring sight to the blind and hearing to the deaf! He came to restore our souls! He says, "And be sure of this: I am with you always, even to the end of the age" (*NLT*, Matthew 28:20). Since He is with us, He can do the same things through us that He did while walking on the earth two thousand years ago!

As my faith for miracles grew, Jesus seemed more close and personal, and I felt like I could trust Him more. Learning that Jesus was doing such tremendous things in my lifetime increased my desire to know Him better and seek Him with an augmented intensity. I realized I would not have to wait until getting to Heaven someday to know Him better. I could pursue and know Him in an authentic way right now!

WE COULDN'T GO WITHOUT IT

We were very aware that if God was calling us to some of the most dangerous parts of Colombia to love some of the most abused people on the planet, we were helpless to make any real change in the lives of these children. They are abused even from the womb, as the mom consumes drugs, gets beaten by her boyfriend, and experiences an entire range of other emotional and spiritual trauma. In addition, after these children are born, many suffer malnutrition, neglect, and every type of abuse imaginable.

After graduating from college with a Bachelor of Arts in Psychology,

I had worked for several years as a social work case manager in Milwaukee. From my experience, I knew that children who undergo such abuse are literally wired differently. Their abusive and negative environment changes the neurons and synapses in their brains. Without the supernatural power of God to heal hearts and bodies and to call His lost children home, we would be powerless to help.

I believe no psychologist in the world can fully heal these children. The best modern science can do for them is to keep them in constant therapy and medicate them for the rest of their lives. We knew that in our own power we were incapable of making any kind of permanent change in this population to which God was calling us.

I cried out to Him, begging, "We *can't* go without You! Don't send us without You! You're the only one who can heal these kids. You *must* come with us in Your power! Don't let us go alone!" In our desperate need for God, we cried out to Him for an entire year. Then we began to sense His presence in new and unexpected ways.

DO YOU REALLY BELIEVE I STILL CAN?

One evening while I was in our den flipping through TV channels, I found a contemporary Christian music concert in which several different bands were performing. Although contemporary Christian music had been around for decades, we hadn't been exposed to it, having attended more traditional churches that played hymns.

During the program, a song came on with lyrics that said something like, "Jesus, the same one who made the blind eyes see and the lame walk...." What happened next took me by surprise, and I still find it difficult to explain. The tangible, holy presence of God came upon me so strongly that it felt as if the air were vibrating with His magnificent presence. It was as if God had just stepped into the room. At the same time a thought began echoing through my mind, asking me, "Tom, do you really believe I still *can* make the blind see and the lame walk?"

I knew this was the Lord speaking to me in what was in reality a whisper, yet it came with such power that it seemed if He spoke any louder, I would not survive. Again came the thought, "Tom, do you really believe I still can? Do you really believe I still can?" Whether or not I believed it, I knew the correct answer. I cried out, "*Yes! Yes!*"

Awed by the power in the room, I asked myself, what does one do in the presence of God? Worship! I fell to my knees with my head pressed into the carpet and worshipped Him with every ounce of my being. As I worshipped, He kept asking me over and over, "Tom, do you really believe I still can? Do you really believe I still can?"

The atmosphere in the basement was so heavy with the holy presence of God that I knew He was there in person. I sobbed, barely able to catch my breath, flooded with intense emotion. I felt pure love, a holy fear of God, and awe that He was speaking to me. It was as if my entire body was vibrating from the inside out. The entire experience unnerved me so much that I struggled to my feet, intending to run away. You've got to understand, nothing like this had ever happened to me before. I didn't know what to do! No one had ever taught me how to respond when the living God shows up in your basement!

As I stood up to run, He spoke to me again, asking, "Tom, do you really believe I still can? Do you really believe I still can?" These words froze me in my tracks. Falling back to the ground in a flood of tears I answered, "Yes! Yes! Yes, Lord, You still can! You still can! I believe You still can! I won't run away. I will stay here as long as You want me. Deal with me however You want!" It's hard to tell how long I was there on the floor in the den...maybe an hour or so. However, when I did get up, I was quite sure about one thing: *God still can and still does heal!*

CONCLUSION

I believe the events in this chapter were divinely orchestrated to awaken our spirits to the realities of Heaven, shake our inner man, and realign our thinking. In order for the Heavenly Father to answer my prayer to draw me closer to Him, He had to correct and change me in many ways. Through this period of "Divine Training," we learned several things.

We learned that God still speaks and that He still heals. We learned to always put our focus and attention on Jesus, and that even when His vision and mission for us are exciting, we must be even more captivated by Him. We learned that God continues to move in astounding ways all around the world, and that we needed to get on board and raise our faith to new levels of belief in what God can do in and through us.

God is on the move, my friends, and *it is exciting*! He's inviting you to be a part of it, but He has one question: do you really believe He still can?

ACTION CHALLENGE

1. Do you want to live an extraordinary life guided by the Holy Spirit? Do you want to exalt Jesus with your life? Then take a moment and ask Him to forgive you for doubting His power and His ability to move in your life.
2. Ask the Holy Spirit to bring to your mind areas in which you need to ask His forgiveness. Then go through the list, asking forgiveness for each item one by one. Commit to following God's plan and His direction for your life, no matter where it leads.
3. Open your heart and ask God to show you any area in which your perspective or understanding of Him is wrong. Ask the Heavenly Father to awaken your spirit to Him and His realities.
4. Journal what you are hearing and feeling.

Chapter Seventeen

3, 2, 1...ACTION!

"Plans fail for lack of counsel, but with many advisers they succeed" (NIV, Proverbs 15:22).

We had worked hard to create the best plan possible for our upcoming missionary work in Cartagena, Colombia, and had spent over a year raising funds for our family. Now just a few months before leaving, we planned to rent our house out to some close friends. They were a couple with three teenage girls who babysat our small children. The girls were homeschooled, and the family was very involved in a local church, with their entire social and support network found there.

A TRAGEDY

One day seemingly out of the blue this family suffered a horrific tragedy. The father became captivated and captured by pornography and abandoned his family for a much younger woman. His wife was a stay-at-home mom with health problems, no college degree, and few means to provide for the girls. She was now stuck with the mortgage, food, and medical payments for herself and her three daughters.

The father was somehow able to get both the local church leadership and his wife's family to believe she was to blame, causing her entire support network to turn against and abandon her and the girls. It's inconceivable how something like this could happen in the body of Christ, but it did.

The wounds were deep in this mom and her girls, and their loss was significant. While the mom lost her husband and all of her friends, the teenage daughters lost not only their father, who no longer seemed to care about them, but their church friends as well.

STAND IN THE GAP

At the time I was still working as a computer engineer at a local hospital. While pondering this crazy situation at work one day, trying to figure out what had happened in the heart of this man and those who had abandoned the mom and girls, the thought crossed my mind that the mom may have done something to cause all of these problems. At that point God's still small voice spoke to me, saying, "You must stand in the gap for her."

I asked, "How can I do that? I don't even understand the situation!"

He continued, "You must love her."

"But aren't we just months away from going to Colombia?" I resisted. "Shouldn't I focus on loving the children in Colombia?"

He answered, "You must love the one in front of you right now, and that is this family. You must love them ridiculously. *You must stand in the gap.*" As God spoke, I understood what He was asking. I must do everything in my power, without reserve, to love and help this hurting family.

Standing in the gap also sounded somewhat Biblical. Supposing that if I could find it in the Bible, it would help confirm God's direction, I searched until I found a passage in Ezekiel which says, "I looked for someone among them who would build up the wall and stand before me in the gap on behalf of the land so I would not have to destroy it, but I found no one" (*NIV*, Ezekiel 22:30).

God is often looking for people to stand in the gap but doesn't always find someone willing to do it. It wasn't God who was trying to destroy this family, but the destroyer, the devil. God wanted someone to fight for them! After consulting with Jen, who was in total agreement, I picked up the phone and called the mom, telling her that our family would stand in the gap for her. I pledged our unconditional support for her and the girls, whatever they needed.

I said, "If you need a best friend, Jen will be your best friend. If you need a father for your children, I'll be that father. If you need a place to live, you can all move in with us. If you need money, a car, prayer... everything we have is yours. We will be there for you!" From a place of unconditional love, Jen and I poured all we had into this dear family. For a time, they did move into our house, and we spent many late nights with them praying, interceding, crying out to God, shedding tears together, and walking hand in hand through this tragedy.

Although the family's situation seemed to worsen before it got better, we saw the hand of God move in extraordinary ways in impossible circumstances, strengthening the faith of all of us. Although those were tough times, God was at the center of it, and our lives were made so much richer by pouring out our love ridiculously.

GIVING UP CONTROL

After getting married, we'd been involved with several churches, one of which was the small family church in which we were new members. Another was the largest church in the city, which we often attended for Bible studies and other events. Many of our lifelong friends attended it as well. The pastor of our small church had agreed to send us out as missionaries, although the church had little experience with missions.

Knowing we needed a solid plan in order for our mission work to be successful, we put together a small team of advisors from our church and the community. These were leaders with wise and gentle hearts who we knew would help to guide us. The committee had been meeting for about six months and we were now just about two months from leaving. I began our meeting one Sunday afternoon by asking the Holy Spirit to take over not only the meeting but also the entire project of sending us. Little did I imagine what would happen as a result of that short prayer!

Minutes later, the head pastor spoke up, appearing surprised that we were planning to leave just a few months later. He'd been thinking it was the following year. He also revealed some anxiety about sending us, saying he didn't know us well enough and wasn't prepared to send us.

Although this came as quite a shock, his concerns were logical. This pastor was from a more traditional background, and he knew we were having significant experiences with the Holy Spirit in healings, words of knowledge, etc. In truth, he wasn't all that comfortable with us not representing what he believed about these workings of God.

On our end, we didn't want to suppress or squash what we believed was the hand of God moving in our lives. We were also very aware that if we went to some of the most dangerous areas of Colombia *in our own power*, we would be helpless to incur real change without the supernatural power of God to heal hearts and bodies, and to call His lost children home.

We had several more meetings with the pastor in which we explained our hearts, goals, and experiences. Although he became much more comfortable sending us, we became uncomfortable with the idea of being sent out by a church that in a year or two may change its mind and call us off the field.

We were now just weeks from our planned departure date and were considering leaving our sending church. However, we didn't want to hurt the body of Christ or do anything without direct confirmation from God. This whole situation threw quite a wrench in our plans, because we were well aware that we needed to be part of a local church that would support us as we went to Colombia. It takes the whole body of Christ to expand the Kingdom of God, and we had no desire to be mavericks or head out on our own.

YOU'VE WORKED REALLY HARD; NOW WATCH ME WORK

With all of this in mind and knowing that we were at a serious crossroads, Jen and I sat down one night with considerable motivation to seek the Lord in prayer. Like two six-year-olds on Christmas day expecting to find presents under the tree, we sat for several hours in expectation waiting to hear God's voice and direction. After a while, I asked Jen if she'd heard anything.

"No," she answered, a bit discouraged.

"Okay, let's press in and wait a bit longer," I urged. We waited, listening for God to interrupt the silence, yet heard nothing. I finally said, "We will not strive in prayer here, so let's listen again for another minute, and then we'll stop if we don't get anything."

We sat for about one minute more, and then Jen jumped up, shouting, "I got a vision!" With her eyes closed she'd seen a full-color 'video movie' of her hands holding up a dirty old broken clay pot with thin, dead plants hanging out of it. As she held it, God's hands came down and lifted it up and out of her field of vision. Seconds later His hands lowered a beautiful

> *"Jen, I just got the words! God said, 'You two have worked really hard...now watch Me work!'"*

blue mosaic pot brimming with life in its place! Multicolored bright flowers sprang up toward the sky, while vibrant green leaves tumbled down over the edge of the pot.

Right after she explained the vision, a phrase entered my mind, and with excitement I remarked, "Jen, I just got the words! God said, 'You two have worked really hard...now watch Me work!'" We both knew what

He meant. We had given our best efforts to get to Colombia. However, this prophetic vision revealed that our best plans now amounted to a broken clay pot holding a few dried-up dead plants.

The blue mosaic pot represented God's promise to take those broken plans and transform them into an exhilarating work of art which would be the catalyst for transformation in our lives and the lives of countless others. The dazzling flowers represented the radiant beauty and abundant life found in what was to come if we followed God's plans instead of our own plans. This sign from God gave us the peace and confidence to weather the storm we were in and inspired us to continue in confident faith that whatever He had for us would be more wonderful than we could imagine.

It was evident from this vision that we needed to abandon our "best plans" which we'd labored over for two years. That meant leaving our current church, canceling our scheduled move to Colombia, and asking our financial partners to put their gifts on hold as we waited for God's plan to manifest itself.

REALIGNMENT

The next day we began the painful process of calling all of our supporters and asking that they stop their giving. We explained that we'd cancelled all of our plans and were now waiting on God and His plans. This was a gigantic step of faith, but we knew God was in it.

In the meantime, doors were opening up for us at the larger church we'd been involved with for several years. There was no guarantee that they would send us out as missionaries. However, they had many ministry connections in the city and even if we never got to Colombia, we knew we could love and serve those in our city in partnership with this church.

When we told the pastor of the smaller church we believed God was calling us out of his church into another, he responded with grace, blessing us while also encouraging members of his congregation to support us once our new plans to go to Colombia were in place. We didn't want anyone to leave his church because of us, nor did we want to cause any damage, and God worked it all out perfectly. It's hard to leave a church that you've sown into and grown with over the years, yet this was part of the broken pot God was calling us to leave.

EMOTIONALLY EXHAUSTED

After all of this happened, we realized how exhausted we were. So much had transpired in the previous four months. We'd found out that God still speaks and that He wanted to heal us and invade our lives. He'd shown us visions and we'd accompanied our friend and her three teenage daughters through horrible tragedy and abandonment.

During this time my father had passed away, and Jen had been diagnosed with MRSA and later cured with antibiotics and prayer. In the midst of all of this, Jen had been involved in a car accident in which somehow our car lurched forward just before impact, allowing for the car colliding into ours to miss our children in the back seat by inches.

We'd left a church and begun attending another, cancelled our plans to go to Colombia, and were now just starting to breathe and let these crazy life events sink in. Yet with all of this craziness, we had a peace that made no sense. We were beyond thrilled at God's intervention in our plans. After having asked so many times, "When is God going to show up?" there was no longer any question...*He had shown up!*

GOD STILL HEALS

We found out that the missionaries from Mozambique whose book had impacted us would be at a missions conference in Cleveland, just seven hours away by car. Around the same time, one of Jen's longtime friends and college roommates offered to let us use her summer lake cottage for a week of rest. Deciding to combine the two, we packed up the kids and headed off on a lengthy road trip.

The first stop was the missions conference. Coming from a conservative religious background, we sat in the back with our Bibles open, examining all the teachings with a fine-toothed comb and comparing them with God's Word. We didn't want to accept anything that couldn't be backed up by the Bible! We were thrilled to find very solid Biblical teaching backed up by exciting testimonies of God's miraculous power still at work today.

For several months before the conference Jen had been suffering from TMJ-like symptoms in her jaw. It often hurt so much that she couldn't play the trumpet, sing, or even talk without pain, and it was bothering her during the conference. During one session the speaker indicated she felt God wanted to heal the sick. All those needing healing in their bodies should stand up, while those around them should start praying for them. An older woman stood up next to us and said she was struggling with cancer, so Jen stood up and lifted her hand to put it on the woman's shoulder.

The very instant Jen's hand touched the woman's shoulder, Jen felt a blazing heat on both sides of her face, and something like surgery happened on the inside of her jaw starting from the top spiraling downward toward her chin. It came and left in thirty seconds, and in that instant all the pain of the TMJ was gone! She spun around and cried out in astonishment, "I think my jaw was just healed!" As of the writing of this book many years later, the pain has never returned. It was a complete and permanent healing! After that personal experience, we knew God not only *wants* to heal, but that He *does* heal!

CROSSING OVER A BRIDGE

When the conference was over, we headed to our friends' beautiful lake cottage in northern Wisconsin. Pulling into the driveway, we were surprised to find this was no humble cottage in the woods, but a newly-constructed large modern lakeside home. It had comfortable white leather couches, a huge kitchen, an enormous balcony, jet skis, a speed boat, and an outdoor jacuzzi tub, and it was ours for an entire week! After all the crazy events of the past several months, we were thrilled to be able to decompress and spend valuable time with our kids. We also spent a lot of time on the couches reading the Bible, seeking God, and processing the extraordinary journey we had been through.

As we did so, we felt a change deep inside of us...like crossing over a bridge. It was as if we'd gone from a life of reading the Bible and hearing about the amazing lives of missionaries, to *living out* the Bible ourselves as if it were a "pop-up" book! We sensed God not only saying that He still heals the sick and brokenhearted, but that He wanted to heal them *through us*! Although we didn't feel righteous or holy enough to be used by God in this way, He insisted, and we made room for Him to come out of the box into which we had put Him, giving Him free access to do whatever He wanted in and through us.

We were understanding in greater measures how profoundly Christ's blood and His payment cleanses us of our sin and filth. He dwells in us and we in Him. He alone is our righteousness. If His Holy Spirit is in us and we are His legitimate children having access to His presence and the throne of grace, why *wouldn't* He touch others through us? Who were we to deny the work of Christ in and through our lives?

The time spent processing these experiences, combined with our increased faith, allowed us to begin to live out the Christian life in a new way. We became more sold out than ever for Jesus, and as we lived out of His miraculous provision, love, and power, we witnessed His hand moving in extraordinary and supernatural ways.

THE SAME WORKS AS JESUS

The Gospel of John records Jesus saying, "I tell you the truth, *anyone* [emphasis added] who believes in me will do the same works I have done, and *even greater works* [emphasis added], because I am going to be with the Father. You can ask for *anything* [emphasis added] in my name, and I will do it, so that the Son can bring glory to the Father. Yes, ask me for *anything* [emphasis added] in my name, and I will do it" (*NLT*, John 14:12-14)!

I now believe that the greatest works of Jesus are not miracles, signs, and wonders, but His humility and love. Back at this point in our journey, however, we were just beginning to capture the idea that God still moves in miracles, and that He wants to partner with His children to accomplish them. Later, His love and humility would change the core of our hearts forever.

CONCLUSION

In this phase of our "Divine Training," Papa God was teaching us to love the person right in front of us. Although we felt called to the children of Colombia, we were learning that we were called to *love*, whether in Colombia or in our living room. It's that simple! We are to focus on Jesus and love the person in front of us wherever we are at any given moment.

We knew this life would be filled with many unknowns. For example, we still had no idea how in the world we would get to Colombia, if ever. We couldn't imagine how this missionary endeavor would be financed or what the future might hold for our family. The only thing we knew for sure happened to be the only thing that mattered to us: Jesus was with us and would continue to walk with us the entire way!

ACTION CHALLENGE

1. Are you making your calling too complicated? We invite you to simply focus on Jesus and love the person in front of you. If you do that, there's no limit to what God will do in and through you!

2. He may be telling you the same thing He told us: "You've worked really hard, now watch me work." Tell Him you are handing Him your "best plans," and want to receive *His* plans for your life instead! Enjoy these moments when you're figuring out the path to God's destiny in your life.

3. God is asking you to step out in faith in at least one or more situations in your life right now. As He talks to you and invites you to put your faith into action, make a note in your journal about which action steps you will take this week.

4. Take the action, and journal with God about your experience.

Chapter Eighteen

MOUNTAINS, FIELDS, AND A TREASURE

> *"The kingdom of heaven is like treasure hidden in a field. When a man found it, he hid it again, and then in his joy went and sold all he had and bought that field" (NIV, Matthew 13:44-46).*

In Heidi and Rolland Baker's book *Always Enough* (Baker, 2003), we read about a pastor named Randy Clark who God used to impact their lives in a most extraordinary way. This pastor still leads many mission trips to Mozambique and Brazil, and three distinct times I felt God nudging us to go on a mission trip to Brazil with his ministry.

I kept this to myself, but when Jen mentioned she sensed the Lord telling her the same thing, we took more purposeful steps to examine if we could take the trip. One requirement for the trip to Brazil was to attend a week of training in Houston, Texas. The other was to read a large ministry manual which would help prepare us.

NEEDING CONFIRMATION

Two things were keeping us from going. First, we knew nothing about Randy Clark and were skeptical about joining an unfamiliar ministry. We would need God's confirmation to go with this new group of people. Second, we had three small children and I was very hesitant to leave them for a week of training and then another ten days to go all the way to Brazil. How could I be certain they were being cared for well? These were my little treasures!

As we examined our possibilities, somewhat stuck in the decision-making process, Jen and I decided we could leave our kids with the mom and three teenage daughters who had been our babysitters for years. We considered them "family" and trusted them with our children. They could move into our house and take care of our kids during both trips. Knowing their financial struggles, we wanted to bless them and decided to give them $1,000 dollars for these two weeks.

Jen and I agreed on this and didn't discuss it with anyone else. However, we still felt that an additional explicit confirmation was needed because the two trips were a huge financial commitment and required significant time off of work for both Jen and me. The cost of the two trips, one to Texas for the training and the other to Brazil, plus the $1,000 dollars for the babysitters, would just about drain our bank account.

It seemed strange that God would send us to Brazil while we still felt called to Colombia. However, God's ways are not our ways, and we would soon find out that His ways are much higher and more excellent than ours! God was not asking us to *understand* His ways, but simply to *trust* Him and *walk* in them. The word *walk* is an action, and when God asks us to walk in His ways or walk out our faith, it requires us to *do* something, to *act* upon the faith He has given us. We must move! In our case, it meant partnering with another ministry for these two weeks.

THE $1,000 CHECK

While awaiting the explicit confirmation that we were to go, I was searching on the internet one Saturday when I discovered that a minister who had traveled with Randy Clark for many years would be giving a conference within a six-hour drive from our home the following week. Since I didn't have any vacation days available, we decided Jen would go to verify that Randy Clark's ministry was legitimate and Biblical, and to seek confirmation for our trip to Brazil.

There wasn't time to register for the event, so Jen drove to Iowa and showed up at the registration desk on Tuesday morning, not knowing anyone. The conference lasted all day, and the speakers were inspiring and Biblically centered. That evening when we talked on the phone, I asked Jen if she had received confirmation, but she hadn't. This was disappointing because I was in such need of clear direction.

On the afternoon of the second day, I took our three kids to the park. As they played, I poured my heart out to God. I said, "Lord, You know I'm not after miracles, signs, and wonders. I'm after You, no matter where You are! If I've been on the wrong track in seeking more of You, Your power, and Your love, that's fine. If it's back to the same old boring church with no miracles, that's fine too, because only You, Jesus, have the words of eternal life. I will follow You anywhere! However, if there *is* a treasure for us in Brazil, we will sell everything we have to buy the field to get the treasure!"

The Bible parable Jesus taught about the man who stumbled upon a treasure in a field that wasn't his own popped into my mind. Jesus taught, "The kingdom of heaven is like treasure hidden in a field. When a man found it, he hid it again, and then in his joy went and sold all he had and bought that field" (*NIV*, Matthew 13:44-46). In our case, the treasure was the Holy Spirit, and we were willing to do whatever was necessary to have Him in plenitude, even if it meant going all the way to Brazil to find Him!

A DRAMATIC CONFIRMATION

While I was at the park with the kids that afternoon, Jen was having an experience that would change the course of our lives. Halfway through the day, a new speaker who had just flown in took the stage and began talking about prophecy.

Then out of nowhere he pointed to Jen in the crowd and said, "The Holy Spirit says you are to continue pouring into the family who has been abandoned by the father and betrayed by everyone they thought they could trust. Also, you have recently gone through a change in churches, but that is good. God is equipping you. You will have a new group of friends and will begin speaking across denominational lines. He is also giving you the gift of healing, and as you use what you have been given, He will give you more. You'll be getting equipped for ministry in a series of upcoming trips."

WOW...*that* was the confirmation we were looking for! Earlier in the day, Jen had invited the other key speaker to go to lunch after the morning session. He was the leader who had traveled many times to Brazil in the past with Randy Clark, and Jen had been hoping to get confirmation through her lunchtime conversation with him. After the morning session ended, a small group of people headed out for lunch, including Jen and the speaker. As she was about to ask what he thought of us going to Brazil, he turned to her and asked, "Does the amount of $1,000 mean something to you?"

Jen shared that it was the price we were planning to pay babysitters in case we went to Brazil. He continued, "God is telling me to give you $1,000. *He says this is the confirmation that you are to go on the trip!*" This minister, who was also a missionary, then gave us a check for that exact amount!

Right after lunch Jen called me on my cell phone, minutes after I had prayed that desperate prayer to God in the park. With great emotion she told me what had happened, and I caught my breath...*this was for me!* God knew how worried I was about leaving our kids behind, and the $1,000 gift was His way of telling me that everything was going to be more than all right!

THE TRAINING WEEK

To prepare for Brazil, we received ministry training in Houston, Texas, for one week in November 2009. They held the training in a large church auditorium, and it included many teaching sessions and opportunities to pray for others. The environment was rather unemotional, with an emphasis on teaching and practical application. With Bibles in hand we focused on the teaching, which to our delight was straight from the Scriptures.

As the week progressed, we saw hundreds of people claiming to be healed of various diseases and conditions during the times of prayer. Although we had recently discovered that God still heals, I remained a bit skeptical. Were *all* of those who claimed to be healed genuine? Were some of them emotional reactions, or even worse, false claims to healing?

CROSSED EYES AND COLORS

Toward the end of the week, one leader sensed that God wanted to heal eyes. I thought of the family sitting behind us with whom we'd chatted throughout the week. Their six-year-old boy, Zack, had severely crossed eyes and wore thick glasses. Could God heal even a serious case like little Zack's?

As a small group of people surrounded the boy and prayed for him, we watched as he slipped to the floor into a restful sleep for about forty-five minutes. When he got up, we all saw that his crossed eyes had *straightened out*! He took off his thick glasses and read literature in his mom's hands, as well as church banners across the room that he couldn't have read before without his thick glasses!

Later that evening, after an hour of Jen and a few others praying for a middle-aged lady who'd been blind from birth, she gained sight for the first time in her life. At first just seeing shadowy figures, with more prayer she began to see objects and even colors. Jen had the amazing privilege of teaching the woman her colors!

THE WOMAN RAISED BY WITCH DOCTORS

Seeing these healings and more on such a large scale increased our faith in God's physical healing. However, He would take us into another realm of learning during that training session, one which we never expected nor desired to enter.

It was late on the last night of the conference. Most of the people had already left while a few remained to attend to those still needing prayer. I was kneeling to pray for an older lady in a wheelchair when from about fifteen feet behind me came a devilish hissing sound that made every hair on my body stand on end. I turned to find a group of people ministering to a lady who was manifesting something straight from hell. Her face, arms, speech, gestures, and body movements were those of some unseen hideous malignant being.

I turned back toward the lady for whom I was praying. My hair standing straight on end, I bowed my head and asked God for two specific things. I begged, "Lord, protect us now, and please give me the necessary training and tools so I will *never again* be so helpless in a situation like this!" God would indeed answer this petition, providing both protection and training for both Jen and me in the near future.

Right after this brief prayer, I moved over to where they were praying for the oppressed woman and witnessed a miracle. One of the ministry leaders was delivering the hissing lady of multiple demons over the course of about half an hour. The process was miraculous, fascinating, thrilling, and terrifying all at the same time. He held the lady's face as a father might place his hands on the cheeks of his daughter. The minister looked into her eyes and spoke her name, trying to keep her engaged and conscious during the deliverance.

Then he called the demons by name and cast them out one by one. When the woman "came to," she had no recollection of what had happened! I later discovered this beautiful Caribbean woman was the daughter of witch doctors and had been cursed through her family. The leader cast many demons out, but then recommended she get further inner healing with a ministry called "Restoring the Foundations International" (RTFI).

INNER HEALING AND DELIVERANCE TRAINING

This experience changed our lives in several ways. First, seeing the enemy manifest in such a real and up-close way confirmed what the Bible teaches as no other teaching could. There is a war, and whether we like it or not, as followers of Jesus we are right in the middle of it! Second, it encouraged us to not only live in holiness but also to remove any demonic influences from our own lives.

Afterwards, we talked to the ministry leader, commenting that we had a call to missions, and he recommended we go through this same week-long inner healing and deliverance ministry ourselves. At first this sounded odd, as neither of us had witch doctors as parents nor were we manifesting any demons. However, he assured us that every person going into full-time ministry of any kind should do this. He himself had gone through it and found it essential.

A few months later, we packed up our three small children and drove across the country to the beautiful Blueridge mountains of Asheville, NC, where RTFI was located. The ministry was so effective that a few months later we returned to receive training as ministers of inner healing and deliverance. I later realized this had been a direct answer to my prayer asking God to give us the tools and training we needed in order to know what to do in that type of situation. God had answered without our even realizing it! He is so kind, gentle, faithful, and good!

THE BAPTISM OF LOVE

With the ministry training behind us, it was time for the trip to Brazil. We ministered every night with the team as prayer ministers, witnessing more healings and deliverances than we ever thought possible in our lifetime.

One particular night Randy announced to the prayer team that there would be a time of impartation. If God was touching anybody on the team during this time, they should continue to receive. Those who were not being touched should pray for others to receive. I thought to myself, "This is the night that God is going to really touch me!" When the time came to receive, I got into position, ready to receive a big download from God.

Eyes closed, feet spread shoulder length apart, hands out with palms facing up, I waited...and waited...and waited. I opened one eye, looking around to see what was happening to everyone else. I closed it and waited some more...but still nothing. After a while I decided that instead of getting disappointed I would just follow the instructions: if you weren't receiving, start praying for others. Going down a line of people who were standing and waiting expectantly, I touched their shoulder or head and prayed for God to touch them.

As I was doing this I began bending over, going lower and lower under the peaceful weight of the presence of God. This was happening, yet I was ignoring it and trying to continue praying for people. Finally, I could no longer stand and dropped to the ground. It felt as if a tangible liquid love was being poured into my innermost being and deep into my soul.

The Lord was pouring out His love in such measure that my only reaction was to overflow with tears and weeping. My nose was running and my face was a mess, but I didn't care...it felt so good to let the tears flow! On the floor I had a vision of Jesus standing over me, smiling while pouring water on me from a big bucket He was holding. This unending water was gushing like a waterfall. Underneath me was a puddle of water from my tears.

This love that poured into me was unlike anything I had ever experienced before. It was so deep, profound, and unending that it immersed every part of my being. As if I were in a warm, deep pool, it poured into me and flowed out in tears. The only way to describe this experience was a baptism of love.

THE FRUIT OF THE BAPTISM OF LOVE

This infilling of the Holy Spirit of God has been one of the principal keys to our ability to survive being on the mission field for so long despite many difficulties. It directly relates to the salvations, lives transformed, leaders developed, and divine miracles we have seen and continue to witness every day. This grace of love He has given me is not my own. It is His, yet it flows through me to touch the lives of those to whom I minister.

I want all of Papa God's sons and daughters to experience this grace of His love, but since it's not mine, I can't give it away. I must implore Papa God to give it to as many as would receive it, and as I've prayed, many *have* received this baptism of love. It has transformed their lives, broken destructive strongholds, helped to put people in ministry and leadership positions, and drawn others into a deep and intimate relationship with God.

KINGDOM THINKING

God has given us extraordinary stories and testimonies which attest to His divine and supernatural intervention. I believe we all have spiritual veils over our eyes which God removes little by little, as we can handle it, throughout our lives. It's only when we die that they will be fully removed and we will see things as they truly are.

We've had the privilege of growing in Him and seeing numerous miracles over the years, and through this spiritual growth process God has taken many veils off of our own eyes. We had to overcome adversities and barriers to learn the lessons needed to experience so many amazing moves of God. We hope you will capture the truths and revelations in these stories so that you don't have to struggle in the same way we did for so long. What took us years to learn or achieve can happen to you in just weeks or months!

The worldly way of thinking says that in order for you to achieve the same things I have, you must put in the same effort, time, and struggle as I did. The Kingdom way of thinking, however, says that I have struggled and put so much time and effort in this process *so that you don't have to*! I can give what I've learned to you, letting my "ceiling" become your "floor." *My top achievement becomes your starting place!*

You will probably achieve more than we have. *We hope you do!* The world's competitive or jealous ways of thinking should never cause Christians to avoid sharing what they have been given with others. Our joint achievements for the Kingdom will be so much greater and impactful than any individual's could be. At the end of the day, the Great God Jehovah will get all of the glory anyway. When Jesus paid for our sins on the cross, He achieved what we could not, and then *He gave it to us for free*! This is Kingdom thinking!

> *When Jesus paid for our sins on the cross, He achieved what we could not, and then He gave it to us for free!*

CONCLUSION

Now that you have read the stories in this book and absorbed the revelations they bring, we want them to put wind under your wings so you can soar higher and achieve even greater things for God. Consider what you might undertake if you knew you couldn't fail. Whether or not you realize it, the Heavenly host is cheering you on! As you step out in faith and wisdom, *you will see and achieve great things for the Kingdom of Heaven*!

It is my deep and heartfelt prayer that everyone reading this book will receive a special impartation from God through His baptism of love. The story of this book has ended, but your story has just begun. Today is a new beginning! This is your day! Now is your time! *The Lord is with you*!

ACTION CHALLENGE

1. Take a moment and hold your open hands out to God. Ask Him to fill you with His baptism of love.
2. As you consider what you might undertake if you knew you couldn't fail, write some ideas in your journal, and then take a practical step toward one or several of them.
3. Continue to journal about your experiences with God.

About the Authors

Thomas and Jennifer Atwater have been living in Medellín, Colombia, since 2011. They have served hundreds of the city's most vulnerable children and families, first as directors of a local children's foundation called Viento Fresco (2011-2018), and now as directors of 911 Life Ministries, which they founded in August 2018. They serve alongside their four amazing children: Alex, Abby, Gabe, and Mariana.

If you would like more information about 911 Life Ministries, please visit www.911life.org or contact Tom and Jen at atwaters@colombiaschildren.org.

Works Cited

i   Fox News. "Medellín 'World's Biggest Brothel'; Sex Trade in Pablo Escobar's Hometown Fueled by Young Virgins." *Fox News*, FOX News Network, 28 Dec. 2016, www.foxnews.com/world/Medellín-worlds-biggest-brothel-sex-trade-in-pablo-escobars-hometown-fueled-by-young-virgins.

ii   Carstens, Cassie. The World Needs a Father: a Trainers' Guide. Cassie Carstens, 2014.

iii McDowell, Josh, and Joshmcdowellministry. "Father Factor Portfolio (Vol 1)." *Issuu*, 2015, issuu.com/joshmcdowellministry/docs/father_factor_portfolio_2015_-_vol.

iv "Study shows loving father is vital for kids' development," The Christian Institute, June 28, 2012, http://www.christian.org.uk/news/study-shows-loving-father-is-vital-for- kids-development/?e290612

v   "A loving father is 'more important to children,'" The Telegraph, June 14, 2012, http://www.telegraph.co.uk/family/9330961/A-loving-father-is-more-important-to-children.html

vi Rebecca Adams, "8 Science-Backed Reasons Why Dads Deserve More Credit", Huffington Post, July 11, 2014, http://www.huffingtonpost.com/2014/07/11/father-child-relationship_n_5558408.html

vii What Does the Latest Research About Fathers Tell Us?" Latest findings presented by Child Trends researchers in "What Policymakers Need to Know About Fathers' in the December 1998 issue of Policy & Practice, the journal of the American Public Human Services Associations (APHSA). www.childtrends.org/n_aboutfathers.asp

viii "Survey Links Teen Drug Use, Relationship With Father." Alcoholism & Drug Abuse Weekly 6 September 1999: 5. "Father Facts," National Fatherhood Initiative, accessed November 21, 2011, http://www.fatherhood.org/father-absence-statistics

ix   Goldman, J., & Salus, M. K. (2003); Buchanan, A.(1996); Calder, M. C., & Peake, A. (2001). Wuertele, S.K., & Miller-Perrin, C. L. (1992). (The Importance of Fathers in the Healthy Development of Children; U.S. Dept. of Health and Human Services; Administration for Children and Families; Administration on Children, Youth, and Families; Children's Bureau; Office on Child Abuse and Neglect; Jeffrey Rosenberg and W. Bradford Wilcox; 2006.

x   Sedlak, Andrea J. and Diane D. Broadhurst. The Third National Incidence Study of Child Abuse and Neglect: "Final Report. U.S. Department of Health and Human Services." National Center on Child Abuse and Neglect. Washington, D.C., September 1996. "Father Facts," National Fatherhood Initiative, accessed November 21, 2011, http://www.fatherhood.org/ father-absence- statistics

xi   https://www.unisabana.edu.co/empresaysociedad/instituto-de-la-familia/ publicaciones/mapa-mundial-de-la-familia/ (Accessed April 15, 2020)

xii   Source: The National Center on Addiction and Substance Abuse at Columbia University. "National Survey of American Attitudes on Substance Abuse VI: Teens." Conducted by QEV Analytics, February 2001. Wade F. Horn, Ph.D. and Tom Sylvester, "Father Facts – Fourth Edition," National Fatherhood Initiative, 2002 National Fatherhood Initiative. – p149

xiii Survey of Teenage girls conducted by Mark Clements Research, as cited in Parade, February 2, 1997. Wade F. Horn, Ph.D. and Tom Sylvester, "Father Facts – Fourth Edition," National Fatherhood Initiative, 2002 National Fatherhood Initiative – p138

xiv   Cunningham, Loren, and Janice Rogers. *Is That Really You, God?: Hearing the Voice of God.* YWAM Publishing, 2010.

xv   Baker, Heidi, and Rolland Baker. Always Enough: God's Miraculous Provision among the Poorest Children on Earth. Sovereign World 2003.